# COMMON GROUND

# COMMON GROUND

## Poets in a Welsh landscape

•

Edited by Susan Butler
Introduced by Anthony Conran

United States distributor
**DUFOUR EDITIONS, INC.**
Booksellers and Publishers
Chester Springs, PA 19425
215-458-5005

POETRY WALES PRESS
1985

POETRY WALES PRESS
56 PARCAU AVENUE, BRIDGEND, MID GLAMORGAN

**British Library Cataloguing in Publication Data**

Common ground: poets in a Welsh landscape.
1. English poetry – Welsh authors   2. English
poetry – 20th century
I. Butler, Susan
821'.914'08   PR8964

ISBN 0-907476-47-3

Design by Anita Boyd

*The publisher acknowledges the financial support of the*
*Welsh Arts Council*

Typeset by Afal, Cardiff
Printed in Baskerville
by
D. Brown & Sons Limited
Bridgend, Mid Glamorgan

# CONTENTS

Foreword . . . . . . . . . . . . . . . . . . . . . . . . . . . . . . . . . . . . . . . . . . . . . . . 7

Introduction by Anthony Conran . . . . . . . . . . . . . . . . . . . . . . . 11

*POEMS AND PHOTOGRAPHS*

ROLAND MATHIAS

    A Letter from Gwyther Street . . . . . . . . . . . . . . . . . . . . . . 21
    Freshwater West Revisited . . . . . . . . . . . . . . . . . . . . . . . . . 23
    Burning Brambles . . . . . . . . . . . . . . . . . . . . . . . . . . . . . . . 24
    Fool's Fingers . . . . . . . . . . . . . . . . . . . . . . . . . . . . . . . . . . 27
    Departure in Middle Age . . . . . . . . . . . . . . . . . . . . . . . . . 29
    Brechfa Chapel . . . . . . . . . . . . . . . . . . . . . . . . . . . . . . . . . 31
    The Flooded Valley . . . . . . . . . . . . . . . . . . . . . . . . . . . . . . 35
    They Have Not Survived . . . . . . . . . . . . . . . . . . . . . . . . . . 36
    Porth Cwyfan . . . . . . . . . . . . . . . . . . . . . . . . . . . . . . . . . . 39

ROBERT MINHINNICK

    Hide and Seek . . . . . . . . . . . . . . . . . . . . . . . . . . . . . . . . . . 43
    Native Ground . . . . . . . . . . . . . . . . . . . . . . . . . . . . . . . . . 44
    Grandfather in the Garden . . . . . . . . . . . . . . . . . . . . . . . . 46
    Smith's Garage . . . . . . . . . . . . . . . . . . . . . . . . . . . . . . . . . 47
    The Orchard . . . . . . . . . . . . . . . . . . . . . . . . . . . . . . . . . . . 51
    The Brook . . . . . . . . . . . . . . . . . . . . . . . . . . . . . . . . . . . . 52
    The Boathouse . . . . . . . . . . . . . . . . . . . . . . . . . . . . . . . . . 54
    The Strata: To Llywelyn Siôn . . . . . . . . . . . . . . . . . . . . . . 57
    Sker . . . . . . . . . . . . . . . . . . . . . . . . . . . . . . . . . . . . . . . . . 58
    Rhigos . . . . . . . . . . . . . . . . . . . . . . . . . . . . . . . . . . . . . . . 61

JOHN TRIPP

    In the National Museum . . . . . . . . . . . . . . . . . . . . . . . . . . 65
    Eglwys Newydd . . . . . . . . . . . . . . . . . . . . . . . . . . . . . . . . 66
    Capital . . . . . . . . . . . . . . . . . . . . . . . . . . . . . . . . . . . . . . . 68
    Penarth . . . . . . . . . . . . . . . . . . . . . . . . . . . . . . . . . . . . . . 71
    Scratch farmer . . . . . . . . . . . . . . . . . . . . . . . . . . . . . . . . . 72
    Epitaph at Gilfach Goch . . . . . . . . . . . . . . . . . . . . . . . . . . 75
    Soil . . . . . . . . . . . . . . . . . . . . . . . . . . . . . . . . . . . . . . . . . 79
    A note from Plwmp . . . . . . . . . . . . . . . . . . . . . . . . . . . . . 80
    At Bosherston Ponds . . . . . . . . . . . . . . . . . . . . . . . . . . . . 83

## GILLIAN CLARKE

Letter from a Far Country . . . . . . . . . . . . . . . . . . . . . . . . . . . . . . . . 87
The Water Diviner . . . . . . . . . . . . . . . . . . . . . . . . . . . . 104
Buzzard . . . . . . . . . . . . . . . . . . . . . . . . . . . . . . . . . . . . . . . 106
East Moors . . . . . . . . . . . . . . . . . . . . . . . . . . . . . . . . . . . 109

## JEREMY HOOKER

Hill country rhythms . . . . . . . . . . . . . . . . . . . . . . . . . . . . . . 113
Beidog . . . . . . . . . . . . . . . . . . . . . . . . . . . . . . . . . . . . . . . . . 114
Brynbeidog . . . . . . . . . . . . . . . . . . . . . . . . . . . . . . . . . . . . . . 117
The mason's law . . . . . . . . . . . . . . . . . . . . . . . . . . . . . . . 118
Wind blew once . . . . . . . . . . . . . . . . . . . . . . . . . . . . . . . 121
Common land above Trefenter . . . . . . . . . . . . . . . . . . . . 122
Shepherd . . . . . . . . . . . . . . . . . . . . . . . . . . . . . . . . . . . . . . 124
As a thousand years . . . . . . . . . . . . . . . . . . . . . . . . . . . . . 126
Leaving . . . . . . . . . . . . . . . . . . . . . . . . . . . . . . . . . . . . . . . . 128

## NIGEL JENKINS

Maidenhair . . . . . . . . . . . . . . . . . . . . . . . . . . . . . . . . . . . . 134
First calving . . . . . . . . . . . . . . . . . . . . . . . . . . . . . . . . . . . 137
The ridger . . . . . . . . . . . . . . . . . . . . . . . . . . . . . . . . . . . . 139
Snowdrops . . . . . . . . . . . . . . . . . . . . . . . . . . . . . . . . . . 141
Goat's Hole, Paviland . . . . . . . . . . . . . . . . . . . . . . . . . . . 148
Castell Carreg Cennen . . . . . . . . . . . . . . . . . . . . . . . . . . 150
Land of song . . . . . . . . . . . . . . . . . . . . . . . . . . . . . . . . . . 152

## ANNE STEVENSON

Himalayan Balsam . . . . . . . . . . . . . . . . . . . . . . . . . . . . . . 157
Walking Early by the Wye . . . . . . . . . . . . . . . . . . . . . . . . 158
Burnished . . . . . . . . . . . . . . . . . . . . . . . . . . . . . . . . . . . . 159
Green Mountain, Black Mountain . . . . . . . . . . . . . . . . . . 163


INTERVIEWS . . . . . . . . . . . . . . . . . . . . . . . . . . . . . . . . . . 179

Notes and Captions . . . . . . . . . . . . . . . . . . . . . . . . . . . . . 217

Map of South Wales . . . . . . . . . . . . . . . . . . . . . . . . . . . . 222

Biographies . . . . . . . . . . . . . . . . . . . . . . . . . . . . . . . . . . . 223

# Foreword

To describe is to listen, to enter
into detail with this ground
and this ground's labour; to take
and offer outward continuing fruit.

*from* 'The Ridger' by Nigel Jenkins

One's apprehension of landscape, even through the supposed 'objectivity' of the camera is never unmediated. Inevitably, it is conditioned by such factors as cultural myths, historical contexts, conventions of representation, and personal associations. But it would not necessarily be desirable to escape these perspectives even if it were possible to do so; one can only attempt to be aware of their influences, their differing possibilities for distortion or cliché on the one hand, or for their reflection of vital, still living connections on the other. While trying to suggest some shared aspects of a broadly cultural view associated with Wales, this project also tries to avoid the imposition of a single style, poetic or photographic, or of a single set of concerns.

There have been a few books recently combining poems and photographs, but usually they have been a collaboration between one poet and one photographer. Here several different approaches, both visual and verbal, intertwine, and a more complex picture of the Welsh landscape, at turns romantic and ironic, subjective and distanced, is built up. The landscapes are as varied as the concerns and associations of the poets, who have been chosen in part because of the different aspects of experience they address and the different areas of Wales their work relates to. The photographs have varying relationships with the poems; they are not intended to 'illustrate' so much as to re-establish for the reader a sense of contact and immediacy between a poem or elements in it and the contexts, the associations from which the poem has partly grown. The photographs are meant in their relation to the poetry to act as touchstones, whether directly or obliquely. But beyond this, they carry their own kind of information and interpretation. And the subjects, the places involved also assert their distinctive presences, to be dealt with in specifically photographic terms.

How the two possibilities of representation, poetic and photographic, come together has to do with the sympathy of outlook and with a concern for the particularities of individual places, things and experiences. And the conscious use photographically of perspectives derived in part from an affinity with poetry gave the possibility of working in ways that acknowledged attitudes toward the Welsh landscape that were more nearly proper to it. This commitment in turn suggested working through a variety of photographic approaches, rather than reducing the treatment of subject matter to any one dominant style. But it is because of the groundedness, the concern with landscape often found in Anglo-Welsh poetry that a photographic response to the poems seemed viable and relevant to begin with. As Raymond Garlick and Roland Mathias have recently observed (in their anthology *Anglo-Welsh Poetry 1480-1980* ), 'the celebration of particular landscapes, the sense of place, the naming of locations mark many [Anglo-Welsh] poems.' Garlick and Mathias go on to remark that 'moreover, this sense of place is often associated with a sense of time — sometimes a personal past...but more often a national past, the immensely venerable continuity of the history of Wales.' This sense of the past as inextricably bound up with the landscape is an important point, and it is something each poet discovers in a different way. To give examples, for Robert Minhinnick this sense is initially personal and is retraced through a series of private childhood haunts, but some of these places are associated with remembered people and their ways of living, of working, which have now disappeared. The past of Nigel Jenkins also recalls youthful experience, in his case that of farm life on the Gower, but there is also a link with the ancient and prehistoric past in his identification with Paviland Man, discovered last century in a neighbouring part of the Gower. Very different from either of these is Gillian Clarke's attempt to rediscover, among other things, the role of previous generations of women in rural areas of Wales, while Roland Mathias' sense of place reflects a wealth of scholarly knowledge across several centuries of Welsh history. As the only truly urban poet in Wales, John Tripp registers in his poetry changes in values taking place in the urban centres of the south, changes measured in part against the values of more rural environments, both past and present.

However varied the ways these poets as individuals pursue a sense of past and place, it is broadly true of them that this sense does not involve an easy nostalgia or romanticism, but rather a consciously affirmed and persistent effort of rediscovery. There is also perhaps in common amongst them an implicit ideal of a more basic, essentialist way of living, one that emphasizes human relationships and fundamental necessities. But this is hardly surprising against the background of a history in Wales that is primarily rural and poor. This background may foster in some a longing to escape, and it has imposed on many the necessity of making a living elsewhere; but it also affords a perspective of hard clarity from which to question the continuing encroachment of consumerist values.

It is a testimony to the wealth of landscape-related poetry in Wales that we are able to present here only a part of it. A truly representative view would have to take into account at least as many more poets as are included in this volume. One limitation in this respect has been the decision to represent each poet in some reasonable scope in order to allow the reader to enter the world of each individual writer and his or her experience of Wales in a way not usually possible on the basis of only two or three poems. This provides a somewhat different approach to problems of accessibility, and we hope that it makes up in depth and suggestiveness what it might lack in conventional breadth. Besides a belief in the excellence of those poets included, there has of course been the necessary consideration, in this context, of the photographic availability of each poet's work. Because of an obvious danger of misplacing emphasis, we have been concerned to choose writers in whose work there is a central strain of landscape or place-related concerns, in other words, an evident 'groundedness'. Choices have also been influenced by the need to present a range of contrasting poetic voices, as well as a range of contrasting views and landscapes. The non-Welsh poets included, Anne Stevenson and Jeremy Hooker, broaden the perspectives still further; their work, being non-native, attests to the distinctive influences that experience of the Welsh landscape and culture can exert on the sensitive outsider.

If this book deals mainly with the southern half of Wales, this is not only because that is where English language poetry predominates, but also because it is perhaps less familiar photographically than the much-celebrated mountain terrain of the north. However, we are particularly indebted to a North Walian writer, Anthony Conran, one of Wales' foremost literary critics as well as one of her foremost poets. On this occasion he has generously consented to play the former role by providing in his Introduction the cultural background to the poetry without which this project would be fundamentally incomplete.

We are grateful to many people, including friends, relatives and acquaintances of the writers who have kindly given us permission and access to photograph many of the places that appear in this book. Our thanks are due also to the University Museum, Oxford, and to the National Museum of Wales, Cardiff. We would like to thank Poetry Wales Press for their continued encouragement, and the Visual Arts Panel of the Welsh Arts Council for a major grant which has supported the photographic work and enabled us to mount an exhibition of it. Finally, and above all, we are indebted to the poets themselves for their enthusiastic participation in *Common Ground.*

Susan Butler, Newport 1985.

# Introduction

This is primarily a book of confrontations. Poets — in various ways dispossessed — are brought face to face with an ancient landscape. Rosie Waite, Ian Walker and Susan Butler, three photographers, confront them with their own images of that landscape, offering the poetry of the lens to the imagism of the word. Multi-media events are always exacting: sometimes the reader will find the relation between poem and photograph easy and smooth and illuminating; in other cases he will find it more difficult, troubling and tangential. The poets are, in this case, given priority. They are allowed time and space to explain themselves and what they are doing. They are permitted to talk, not just make poems. The photographers — except in a brief foreword — keep their peace. As I say they are offering their images to the poetry. They are, in one sense, standing in for the landscape that the poets are confronting. In another sense, however, and just as truly, they are confronting the landscape as well. They and the poets look at each other across common ground.

That common ground can be more or less identified with Wales: if you want to quibble, Wales south of the Ystwyth, since none of the poets hales from north of that. It *is* a quibble though, because Wales is one country, one landscape, one community. The poets are not regional writers. They refer themselves to a nation, Wales, with its own language, its own history and culture. Glamorgan coal measures and Gwynedd slate are part of a continuum, a geological and social fact of life, a state of mind.

The rocks themselves are old: most of them were laid down a long time before dinosaurs walked the world. They have been raised, buckled, shattered, worn down by water and ice; but they are everywhere a significant part of one's apprehension. Two of them, coal and slate, dominate the recent economic life of vast stretches of the countryside. The rock and its antiquity is forced upon you in Wales — there is hardly anyone whose biography has no reference to it.

Saying that Wales is one country, one landscape, one community, lays you open to attack these days. Two hundred years ago, the argument runs, it was obviously a unified community because everyone — barring a few Englishmen — spoke Welsh, lived in rural, homespun society, was open to the same cultural and religious forces. But now the two languages, Welsh and English, confront each other over every inch of the land; and Welsh seems to be losing the struggle, though it fights back with courage and determination. Two languages, two cultures; are there therefore two countries? I have heard members of the Welsh Language Society deny that Cymru — by which they mean a Welsh-speaker's idea of his country — has much to do with the 'Wales' of the English-speaking Welshman. The problem would then be to divide the two: where does Wales end and Cymru take over? Welsh-speakers for a lot of the time have to use English as a *lingua franca* — are they any less Cymry, people of Cymru? Perhaps they are; but then the division between Cymru and Wales becomes a psychological border, not a social or political one.

The two languages confront each other; and it might be thought that the poets in this book, who of course write in English, would be hostile or at least indifferent to the fate of the Welsh language. In fact these poets are very conscious of the Welsh past. The two outsiders, Hooker and Stevenson, are, to say the least, sympathetic to the culture they have entered, and wish to honour it. The insiders, the poets who come from Wales, in varying degrees feel exiles in their own land. They cannot write in Welsh, and yet there is buried in them a whole continent of assumptions that have their origin in that language and have no organic relationship with English culture. For a poet, many of these assumptions concern the role and nature of poetry. Welsh poetry has been a continuing strength in Welsh life for as long as it makes sense to talk about Welshness at all.

Welsh crystallised out of British Celtic about six or seven centuries before Anglo-Saxon was creolised into English by the Norman-French captivity. To that extent it is an ancient tongue. The Dark Ages, and even Rome, are an implicit part of its cultural luggage. It is quite common to find that Welsh Christian names go back to Arthurian times: Aneurin Bevan for instance was named, at however many removes, after a sixth century Welsh poet. How many English people are called Hrothgar or Beowulf? Welsh survives as the first language of over half a million people, spread throughout Wales but mainly in the West and in the country districts rather than the towns. From the sixth century onwards it has supported a thriving literature, particularly in poetry where it enjoyed a classical age in the fourteenth and fifteenth centuries. In Dafydd ap Gwilym, at any rate, it possesses a love poet of world stature, one of the three or four greatest poets of the European middle ages.

A feature of this literature is that, from the beginning, the poet has been a man with a job to do in his society. While Wales was still an independent collection of petty kingdoms, the poet's job was the ritualistic praise of kings. His praise had a magical, quasi-religious and certainly political function. It was almost felt that you could not be a king at all unless you were praised by a properly qualified poet. When the English king Edward I conquered Wales, this function was lost — there were no Welsh kings to praise. Or at least, it was put in cold storage, for it is arguable that when a Welshman, Henry Tudor, at last won the throne of England in 1485 he owed at least part of his success to the prophecies and praise-poetry of the Welsh poets rousing their people in his support. Be that as it may, however, for the most part Welsh poets were barred from kingship's praise. They had to make do with the gentry. Every Welsh squire and petty aristocrat in the middle ages was praised for his hospitality, his courage, his virtue and his sustenance of Welsh life. The Welsh classical poets had one great theme: the good life as it was lived and as they hoped it would continue in the great houses, defended and made gracious by the open-hearted patronage of the gentry. Love-poetry, and even religious poetry, were produced in quantity but were equally based finally on that one theme. God — or the poet's mistress — had enough features in common with the poet's patron to make praise of either possible within the one tradition. Even when, in due time, the Welsh gentry were almost anglicised out of existence, Welsh poets still remembered that their true function was praise, and their true milieu was the community. To an extent undreamt of in England today the Welsh poet was not — and still is not — alienated from his fellow Welshmen. He writes as part of a community, not as the suffering individual with his *angst* and his desperate subjectivity.

Welsh poetry, then, is orientated towards praise, or its opposite, invective. The first thing one notes about it is that it is praise directed towards, and in support of, consensus. It has not much to do with the voicing of opinion or the agreement to differ that is characteristic of English life. A great Welsh poem invariably moves as if it had the whole community behind it: even the satires, for example of Saunders Lewis, are very like a society undergoing self-criticism. When English people come up against the pressures of consensus, whether at the level of Lloyd George's oratory or at a local council meeting, they tend to be baffled or even angry. Welsh poetry is not necessarily oratorical, of course, but its function of praise works a bit like oratory in that it preserves comradeship and common ground.

The other notable thing about Welsh poetry is that it is a genuinely popular art: indeed, a folk art. The only really national festival Wales has, the Eisteddfod, is many things at once — social gathering, cultural market, competitions in music and art, temporary and movable capital of Wales for one week in August: but the heart of it is a poetry festival. Twice during the week the whole population of the Eisteddfod field waits in silence to hear who has won the crown (for a poem in the so-called 'free' metres) and the chair (for the strict-metre *awdl*, usually translated 'ode' but in fact 'lay' is probably the more accurate term). The crowning, and above all the chairing, form the climax of the whole week; and emotions run high. Not merely that, but one of the most popular places during the week is the *pabell llen*, the literature tent, where discussions and literary events take place. The competitions in poetry are many and various, and hundreds of poets take part, from all walks of life.

To be a chaired poet — bard is the usual translation, but in Welsh *bardd* is simply a poet — is to possess the highest honour Welsh culture affords. It is awarded for a poem in the 'strict metres', the twenty-four traditional metres formulated in the fifteenth century but in fact going back, some of them at least, to the sixth. This is no place to describe them; suffice it to say that they are among the most complicated in the world. One thing one must add, and that is that they do not so much impose a pattern as give the poet a choice of patterns, at every stage of his composition. From twenty-three lines of *cywydd*, for instance, all it is possible to say about the twenty-fourth is that it will have seven syllables and will rhyme (in an off-beat sort of way) with the twenty-third. But no one can forecast the stress pattern or which of the four varieties of alliteration and internal rhyme the poet will use. This combination of extreme complexity and really quite a lot of freedom is typical of Welsh metrics.

Poetry as praise, as a social art and as craftsmanship are the three ways a poet is aware of his art in Wales. But of course, for an English-speaking poet, there are English assumptions as well: poetry in England is largely the art not of praise but of personal viewpoint, not of popular consensus but of individual isolation; and craftsmanship is not a matter of form, primarily, but of style. The English poets of Wales are generally known as the Anglo-Welsh, a term which has often been deplored as a description: it means 'from Wales, in English.' It does not imply any other hybridization than that, nor should it carry any of the customary denigratory suggestions of Anglo-Indian or Anglo-Irish. Anglo-Welsh poets include David Jones, Dylan Thomas, Alun Lewis and R.S. Thomas, and up to the nineteen-sixties constituted a series of brilliant individualists but hardly a tradition: the four poets I have mentioned have extraordinarily little in common with each other. Since the founding of the magazine *Poetry Wales* by Meic Stephens in the middle sixties, however, Anglo-Welsh poets have tended, more or less, to share distinct family characteristics, and most would acknowledge R.S. Thomas as some sort of elder brother. Dylan Thomas, who remains for most outsiders the quintessential Welsh poet, is perhaps admired but not usually influential.

Anglo-Welsh poetry was a comparative latecomer on the scene. It hardly made much impact before the thirties of this century. The gradual anglicisation, spreading from the east, particularly in the mining valleys of the South had by then made great inroads into Welsh Wales; compulsory education in English had created a literate audience for Anglo-Welsh writing. Even so, short story and novel preceded by some decades the growth of a poetic movement. At first poets like Dylan Thomas and Alun Lewis tried to compete on the English poetry scene: the end of this expansionist, rather swashbuckling and experimental phase, full of the 'lovely gift of the gab', more or less coincided with the death of Dylan Thomas in 1953 and the success of his play for voices, *Under Milk Wood*. Then the mood of Wales — or at least English-speaking Wales — changed: before 1953 it was dominated by the inter-war Depression in all its misery and heroism, and by the need to escape. The Welsh language was associated with poverty and the past. Dylan Thomas, for example, showed very little regret that it seemed to be dying, and made fun of Welshness even if he did so with affection. But a new nationalism was stiffening the resistance of Welsh Wales even before the war: and by the fifties and sixties this was affecting the English-language writers as well, in particular the poets R.S. Thomas and Harri Jones and the novelist Emyr Humphreys. To write about Wales for a London or English market imposed more and more strain on writers, because the temptation to exploit English stereotypes of Welshness interfered with creative seriousness. In any case, English fashion turned away from Anglo-Welsh genre-writing. The poets started to write for a market in Wales — if the English liked them, well and good, but at least some of them were writing primarily for their own countrymen.

The creation of such a market within Wales has not, unfortunately, been markedly successful, even though latterly it has enjoyed a great deal of support from the Welsh Arts Council. English-speakers in Wales, for the most part, do not differ much in their literary tastes from those in Durham, Surrey or Devon. If they buy books at all they tend to buy what the London market spreads before them, with only a sprinkling of 'local' publications. Even R.S. Thomas would not have been bought on any scale in Wales had he not first been promoted and taken up in London. This has resulted in a three-tier culture in Wales as a whole. First, English literature, journalism, radio and television, radiating from London, spreads its mid-Atlantic and other lesser subcultures over all of Wales, but particularly over English-speaking districts. Secondly, the ancient and separate culture in the Welsh language, with its own publishers, radio and now television channel. And thirdly, a second English literature, that of the Anglo-Welsh, trying to protect and cherish its own tiny market in Wales and to offer a Welsh alternative to official English culture. Anglo-Welsh writing is clearly in a very ambiguous position. Linguistically it is identified with English mass culture as it erodes Welsh values slowly away, but economically and (on the whole) ideologically it is a poor relation and would-be ally of Welsh-language culture and literature.

The conservationist aspect of Anglo-Welsh poetry since the sixties has been matched, of course, by similar movements elsewhere, both in Britain and overseas. Hooker and Stevenson, one from England and the other from America, both found they could support and sympathise with a great deal of

Anglo-Welsh aspiration. Where it differs from English movements is in its cultural nationalism and its divided inheritance, one half from pan-English culture, the other from its sister literature in Welsh Wales. And whereas to Hooker and Stevenson the presence of this popular, unalienated poetry in Welsh acted as a release and a stimulus, to the Anglo-Welsh it was often a sign of their own disenfranchisement and guilt at forsaking the ways of their fathers.

The position is complex, and I am afraid that this introduction over-simplifies at almost every point. But perhaps it will provide some kind of scaffolding, not too wildly misleading, for the relative outsider to approach these poets, the pressures they have registered and the achievements of their art.

It is time to return to the poems and landscapes. As Susan Butler once remarked in a letter to me,

> "landscape is a focal issue in Wales, and not just in poetry, because it is the obvious thing that Welsh people in general can identify with, whatever their original tongue. In a very real sense, it could be said that landscape *is* the face of a culture, and will necessarily reflect its changes, even while persisting beyond them."

It is in this faith that she, Ian Walker and Rosie Waite have planned and executed this book. I wish it the success it deserves.

Anthony Conran

# ROLAND MATHIAS

# A Letter from Gwyther Street

This morning, the rain pucker over,
I crossed Barafundle from the sun rocks
To the leaf bank westward. It was fine
And feathery on the uppish wave. My feet
In lifting sand uncovered an older
Sun and a captured wind dry-beached a decade
Ago. But this is October, the salted-down
Summer of the deckspar, colloped by sea-
Worms, and the indestructible layabout
Plastic of the child engineer.

This evening, such brief spirit sinking, I visit
Friends. And first to the grave-spit at Llanion
Where Sian, her W.V.S. uniform in full
Fold, pairs her ankle-bones to town. Is there
A message for Elis, tied to his cot like
An idiot, his delicate features clouded
Towards a bad-weather eye? Or Doc, cooped up
With his leg off? Or Herbie, lopsidedly
Smiling in the front room, omnivorous,
History and egg slapped on unknowing cheek?

My footprints this morning on Barafundle
Went in and out of the wave, the fine sand
Darkening at the tide-touch and, as I looked back,
Not a mark of my passing anywhere, only
Sea eating the whiter sift, creaming mouthfuls
Of stick and hampered stone and memory
Trapped there. What remains of companionship
Cannot reach them now, Herbie and Doc
And Elis. No eye-light flickers and signals
Identification on their already buried beach.

# Freshwater West Revisited

After six years this winter has not changed,
Encounter of sea and land, ellipses
Of force that intersect and flow boldly
Into and round each other as though
The air were party to either, *socius*
Only because savage both determine so.

This is no place of secondary forms,
Pretty distractions, heights of cliffs
Or trees, not far-out ships puffing
Irrelevantly of other shores and clashes.
Here the brute combers build the waterhead
And grass girds up the dunes the shock washes.

Away inland one can forget so much,
Ease the elliptical abrasions, bandage, duck,
Sidestep the bull-nosed rushes of a wrong
On right, proffer a parody to the back of it.
This cold October morning lays the action bare:
Sea is, and land, and bloodwreck where they meet.

# Burning Brambles

The sea at a distance glints now and again, as though
This upland corner, puzzled with smoke, had a new heart to show.

But the land is unhealthy, smelling of green-cut bramble
And rotting sticks; bumps in it, bare of all grass, resemble

Boils that the bold rooting whips had crossed, lanced once of their pus
And left, foetid and out of sight. It is an old covert, the fuss

Of discovery long muted: in the back ditch the tins are so many
Rust-flakes that part in the fingers, dusting on black bottles rainy

Yet stoppered, a heap of old sins without consequence, save
Deep in the land's heart where the sods of the field wall gave

Them summons for turbulence. And now there is burning, sullen
Bramble whips dragged a while since to their pyramid, crestfallen

But free to strike and trip as they can. The one fire catching,
Out of the gusts from the north-west, needs that quick watching

That one cannot give who forks and carries recalcitrant
Loops from the pyre lower down, full in the wind, only intent

On freeing himself and not falling, with the burdened fork
Wide of the body. It is a slow excoriation: the whips work

Back on the hand, mindless as snakes but bitter. And the smoke
Is bitter, making the nose run and the freer arm for its soak

Keep a shirt-cuff handy. Even the flames bite back, leaving
The near scalp smoked and the green rotten smell of the stalks waving

Threats overhead. The clog of leaves and sticks must be left
Momentarily on the ground. It is enough to unpile and shift

The endless loops of this waste, hearing the crackle behind
And knowing the smell of a life ill lived as it passes down wind.

# Fool's Fingers

Not everything is named, either
For memory's sake or for the marks
In the book. And what's most secret,
Ridiculous in its fashion, has
Often no more of date than
Repeated omens, settings of twigs
Or stones, threatening the week
With another dervish appearance.

There had been snow that the noon
Sun melted. The sloping fields
Still had a snow-rash, the roughest
Grass clumps sparkily topped with white.
The nameless runnel that lower down
Brings a stick or two to Soar's
Unheeding backs like a wet bitch
Shaking herself dropped here
Suddenly through a culvert from left
To right of the road. The walled-in roar
It was pulled me, from habit, to peer
Down at the wintered split channel
And there, all but surfing the small
Blurt of water, hung a line of daredevil
Ice-shapes, onions, pears, inverted cold
Parsnips of ice that the bank's
Promiscuous trickles had dripped faster
Than one frost's icicles. Down
To the very tips they had run
To freeze, these water-joints, these
Drips without knuckles, pompously fived
And bladdered to make fool's fingers —
Not Struwwelpeter's with trumpery nails
But fat shilling digits with the heart's
Cold water blue in the ends. Later
I saw them everywhere, under the field's
Cornice, solemnly hung from a tree-root
Close to the shock of free water
But never quite carried away.
                                          I doubt
That the day will stand, but the image
Will, as my heart fidgets off, gloving
Fool's fingers with a different colour.

# Departure in Middle Age

The hedges are dazed as cock-crow, heaps of leaves
Brushed back to them like a child's hair
After a sweat, and clouds as recently bundled
Out of the hollows whimper a little in the conifers higher up.
I am the one without tears, cold
And strange to myself as a stepfather encountered
For the first time in the passage from the front door.

But I cannot go back, plump up the pillow and shape
My sickness like courage. I have spent the night in a shiver:
Usk water passing now was a chatter under the Fan
When the first cold came on. They are all dead, all,
Or scattered, father, mother, my pinafore friends,
And the playground's echoes have not waited for my return.
Exile is the parcel I carry, and you know this,
Clouds, when you drop your pretences and the hills clear.

# Brechfa Chapel

Not a shank of the long lane upwards
Prepared our wits for the myth, the slimed
Substantiation of the elements. And the coot
With his off-white blaze and queasy paddle
Was an old alarm, the timid in flight
From the ignorant. The lowered shoulder
Of mountain it is, dabbled within the collar,
That shallows and darkens the eye, the first
Slack argent losing the light as bitterly
As the blackened water treads and nibbles
The reeds and bushes afloat in the new
Pool's centre. Beyond, a surviving ray
Points and fondles a reed-knot, the swan
That dreams on it taking no note of stumps
Or visitations. Nearer, however, and shifting
Like pillagers from weed to shore, settling
And starting raucously, hundreds of testy
Black-backs utter their true society, bankrupt
Hatred of strangers and bully unrest whichever
Marge they think themselves forced to. It
Is a militant brabble, staked out by wind
To the cropped-down pasture. Mud and the tricky
Green of the edge contrivingly clap it round
What's left of this latish day that began with love.

Opposite, to the west of the harsh lagoon,
Stands a chapel, shut in its kindred wall
With a score of graves. Legend on one
Cries a minister, dead of the heats in Newport
Before he came twenty-eight, his wife
Rambling on to her eighties. On another a woman
Loosens at thirty, her man afield on the mission
Ploughing till dark. O these stones trouble
The spirit, give look for look! A light from this
Tiny cell brisked in far corners once, the hand held
Steady. But now the black half-world comes at it,
Bleaks by its very doors. Is the old witness done?
The farmers, separate in their lands, hedge,
Ditch, no doubt, and keep tight pasture. Uphill
They trudge on seventh days, singly, putting
Their heads to the pews as habit bids them to,
And keep counsel. The books, in pyramid, sit tidy
On the pulpit. The back gallery looks
Swept. But the old iron gate to the common,
Rusted a little, affords not a glimpse
Of the swan in her dream on the reed-knot
Nor of the anxious coot enquiring of the grasses.
The hellish noise it is appals, the intolerable shilly-
Shally of birds quitting the nearer mud
For the farther, harrying the conversation
Of faith. Each on his own must stand and conjure
The strong remembered words, the unanswerable
Texts against chaos.

# The Flooded Valley

My house is empty but for a pair of boots:
The reservoir slaps at the privet hedge and uncovers the roots
And afterwards pats them up with a slack good will:
The sheep that I market once are not again to sell.
I am no waterman, and who of the others will live
Here, feeling the ripple spreading, hearing the timbers grieve?
The house I was born in has not long to stand:
My pounds are slipping away and will not wait for the end.

I will pick up my boots and run round the shire
To raise an echo louder than my fear.
Listen, Caerfanell, who gave me a fish for my stone,
Listen, I am alone, alone.
And Grwyney, both your rivers are one in the end
And are loved. If I command
You to remember me, will you, will you,
Because I was once at noon by your painted church of Patricio?
You did not despise me once, Senni, or run so fast
From your lovers. And O I jumped over your waist
Before sunrise or the flower was warm on the gorse.
You would do well to listen, Senni. There is money in my purse.

So you are quiet, all of you, and your current set away
Cautiously from the chapel ground in which my people lie ...
Am I not Kedward, Prosser, Morgan, whose long stones
Name me despairingly and set me chains?
If I must quarrel and scuff in the weeds of another shire
When my pounds are gone, swear to me now in my weakness, swear
To me poor you will plant a stone more in this tightening field
And name there your latest dead, alas your unweaned feeblest child.

# They Have Not Survived

They have not survived,
That swarthy *cenedl*, struggling out
Of the candled tallut, cousins to
Generations of sour hay, evil-looking
Apples and oatmeal porringers.
A quick incontinence of seed
Cried in the barn, a mind to spit
And squat harried the gorse
Into burning, and the melancholy
*Rhos* burst into plots, as circumscribed
Only as the lean muscle yearning
Carefully for love could lay
Around each house. But of that
Merely a life or two, enough to multiply
Cousins like bloodspots in the wasted
Grass. Then a new swarmimg, under
An aged queen, before they walked
Their milgis over the ragged hill
They ghosted every shift, farming
A memory of that last-seen
Country that was never theirs.
It was not will was lacking then
So much as instinct, a gift
Of seed for their backyard culture,
A grip on the girl who bears.

They have not survived.
Coughing in terraces above
The coal, their doorsteps whitened
And the suds of pride draining
Away down the numbered
Steps to the dole, they denied
Both past and future, willing
No further movement than the rattle
Of phlegm, a last composure
Of limb and attitude.
For this dark cousinhood only I
Can speak. Why am I unlike
Them, alive and jack in office,
Shrewd among the plunderers?

# Porth Cwyfan

June, but the morning's cold, the wind
Bluffing occasional rain. I am clear
What brings me here across the stone
Spit to the island, but not what I shall find
When the dried fribbles of seaweed
Are passed, the black worked into the sandgrains
By the tide's mouthing. I can call nothing my own.

A closed-in, comfortless bay, the branchy
Shifts of voyage everywhere. On a slope
Of sand reaching up to the hidden
Field or stretch of marram a tipwhite, paunchy
Terrier sits pat on his marker, yapping me
Bodily out of range. What in God's name is he
Guarding that he thinks I want of a sudden?

To the left is the island, granite-hulled
Against the froth, the chapel's roof acute
As Cwyfan put it when the finer
Passions ruled, convergent answers belled
Wetherlike towards God. Ahead is the cliff
Eaten by sand. On the quaking field beyond
Low huts, ordered and menacing. Porth China.

Once on the island those last shingle
Feet I came by seem in threat.
Can you, like Beuno, knit me back severed
Heads, Cwyfan, bond men to single
Living? Your nave has a few wild settles
And phantasmagoric dust. And Roger Parry,
Agent to Owen Bold, has a stone skew-whiff in the yard.

Doubling back again is a small
Inevitable tragedy, the umpteenth
In a sinuous month. Now I avoid
The violent pitch of the dog, with all
And nothing to guard, remark his croup,
The hysteric note in the bark. Two dunlin,
Huffing on long legs, pick in and out of the tide.

A man on the beach, a woman
And child with a red woollen cap,
Hummock and stop within earshot,
Eyeing my blundering walk. 'Can
We get to the island?' he asks, Lancashire
Accent humble, dark curls broad. And I
Am suddenly angry. But how is my tripright sounder,
Save that I know Roger Parry and he does not?

# ROBERT MINHINNICK

# Hide and Seek

The damp mahogany shade
Between chapel and the terraces
Concealed a territory
I thought only we children knew.

Bindweed spread its bitter
White rosettes over headstones, the dew
Gleamed like porcelain in the stillness
As I listened for my friends to come

And find that hiding-place —
Under the hogweed where the graves
Were thrown open like drawers
And snails unwound their silver

On my jersey; under the hogweed
With the dead in their dormitory.
But awaiting a crackle of voices
I knew even then it would not be

Friends that found me out,
Or set me running from that
Startling intimacy, the yellow
Stitched cranium, the opening pit.

# Native Ground

In my grandparents' home the weekly treat
    Was the hard globe of a pomegranate.
With the juice on my chin I would watch
    The woman rinsing pans, scabs on her
Knuckles and the fat yellow wedding-ring

Gleaming in dishwater. Every day
    Of her life she would submerge with those pots,
Throwing the gossip over her shoulder
    In an ugly jewellery of words
I had not learned to value. What was she

Talking about all the time? The names
    And the proverbs were strange as the rind
Of the pomegranate, that difficult fruit.
    So I fumbled with its scarlet honeycomb
And stared through the window at my grandfather,

Bent it seemed permanently towards the earth,
    Always the man apart, but scrabbling now
With the creeping flower called pimpernel
    Scattered everywhere like confetti.
And then I would turn and yawn and listen;

And listen, pinpricking the jewels
    Of the pomegranate, not wondering about
History, that tangible subject I might love.
    There and then I was happy, if bored.
And time added another piece to the mosaic.

# Grandfather in the Garden

Digging was always my worst work.
After ten minutes I would blow
My scalding hands and watch him fork
Quite effortlessly the rain-heavy clay
Of a new garden, meticulous and slow
Labour that soon tired a boy.

All his life a cultivator
Of the soil's best things, ingenious
Exterminator of what opposed his sure
Design. Summers wet or dry found him
Aware of deep conspiracies of earth
To damage or destroy the year's triumph.

Thus he squared his jaw, donned ancient
Clothes, and set to digging out his
Fears. Late evenings I'd be sent
To call him in, a dark and elemental
Shape by then, the ruins of a young man's face
Still visible behind the years, the toil.

A labourer and architect,
He taught patience in slow lessons
And one man's dedication to a craft.
From his cracked hands I watched the brittle seed
Cast surely for the future, the unborn;
Those acts of affirmation his deep need.

# Smith's Garage

After the death of memory
Everything is strange.
What was treacherous
Becomes the way of life.

Gone the hammer strokes
And the saw's musical
Friction; the generator
Droning like a hive.

All the voices raised
To counterpoint the discords
Of the lathe proved a close
Association undermined.

Only ivy's industry
Survives the change. New season's
Growth crowds the skylight's
Pale tonsure of glass.

A lorry chassis burnt
With violent rusts
Finds irreducible bone-like
Fusions with the earth.

How we knew ourselves
Was how we laboured;
Turned to touchwood now
That busy cell of work.

# The Orchard

Existing no longer, its loss becomes
A lasting recollection, clear, acute.
Apples so hard they would bleed the gums,
Greengages bottle green and fierce as gin.
How the mouth would twist over that stolen fruit,
The sour exhilaration of that sin.

# The Brook

Infamous for eels, bearded, wrist-thick,
Some wound like electric cable round a gaff,
Their truncheon heads thrusting at the air.
How cold they were, vicious, familiar;
Generations coiled together on bright gravel.

But because they grew so great I'd devil
Myself to wade upstream, thinking of eels
Black and vulcanized like bicycle tyres
Knotting my legs, my drowned face with the eyes
Eaten. Tree roots waving in the current.

Then my mind was like the stream's ferment
Of lives, the water round the carcase of a steer
Disturbed by the invisible, the secretive
Come to feast. But if the brook was death's element,
The harmless eels were the evil I'd invent.

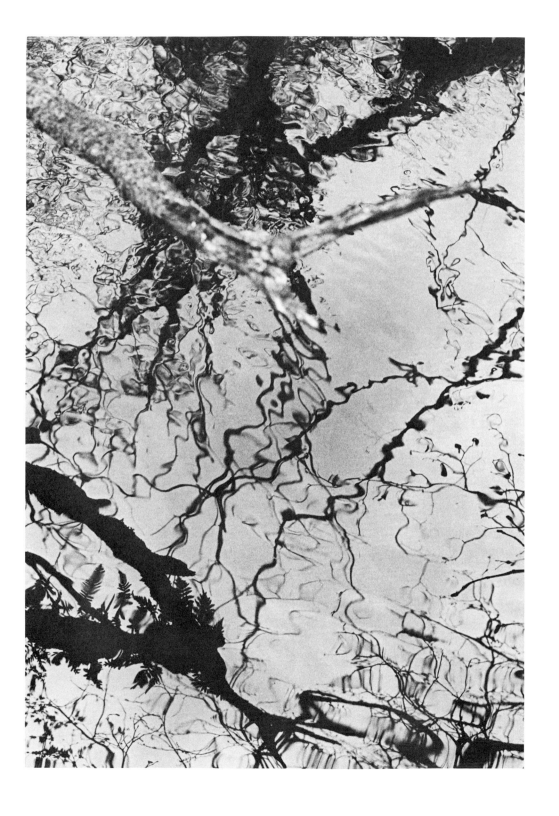

# The Boathouse

The sawyers lie outside the shed,
Their blades motionless for the first
Time today, the men silent, sprawled
On a floor of white dust, their
Haversacks before them, and behind,
The heaps of sawn wood, the logs stacked
Like new loaves, the smell as sweet.

In my mind they will sit there forever,
The village men in feudal grouping,
Craftsmen of the estate, and my mother
Saying 'Good morning sir' to the gentleman
As he passes, to the brassy heads
Of cartridges in his twill. A smile
For the girl remembered always.

It's finished now. The whole place
Closed down. Employment's found outside
The creamery, the vinery and grange
Farm that fed inherited wealth,
That tiny, epic world once sufficient
To itself, working perfectly and
Observed from the boathouse by this

Trespasser hidden amongst anglers'
Tackle, the moss-coloured lake sliding
Under the boards. Suddenly everyone
Had fallen asleep — nurserymen,
Chauffeurs, kitchenmaids — the hour
Went unstruck. There was nothing
But silence and the soft putrescence

Of the boathouse, the shoals of ochre
Mud where water stood. Through a rotten
Lath the lake slipped in; the vans arrived,
I heard the barking of the country
Auctioneers, 'Good morning sir
Sir sir' of my mother talking to the dead,
A population slamming doors on a way of life.

# The Strata: To Llywelyn Siôn

Llywelyn, jackhammers ring in unison
At the gate. The ribs of monastery
    And fulling mill must collapse through thorn.
    It's an open grave, this house where you were born.

And shameful, the discoveries of time.
Sunlight pours into the privy-slot
    Black as the century that laid your faith.
    Llywelyn, this cloister smells of death.

Yet I know I have seen in faint rushlight
A man grow hunchbacked over a poem
    Before stretching into sleep's luxury,
    His pool of ink unblinking, a dark eye

That follows me six hundred years later
Through the thin woods of Llangewydd.
    Poet, you will understand my body's thirst
    As from this ground I watch unearthed

A cross like a cloverleaf incised in granite,
A markstone, a boundary of fear
    And belief. And clearly at once I see
    The strata, the separate rings of the tree

Of time, each growing from the last.
Llywelyn, living man, this is my history lesson,
    An instant's shocked discovery
    That I am able to claim what is mine,

To fashion with blunt words my own design
Of the cross. All we need is the courage
    To look around and we will find our own
    Mythology. Here, on native ground.

## Sker

Everywhere the sea, pungent as mustard.
We come over the ploughland to the dunes
And realize this is all we know
Of wilderness — scarps rising like
Marram-green combers at the tide's
Fringe, their waves inching towards
The waves in the glacial progress of sand.

A hawk, a dunghill, the concrete foxholes
Made for war. Christ, the wind cuts,
It cuts right through. Before history
We are naked children not seeing
The storm, climbing over the rusted
Wire of the gun-range while the sea's
Artillery crashes overhead. We run

Ignorant of our ignorance, trampling
Through the burnt tapestry of gorse —
A patch of sunlight a moment's absolution —
Down to Sker, down headlong to where
The dunes lie between the bay and red
Potato fields, where the house, great
Medieval wedge, stands fused by weather

And memory to the skyline. Here on
The Viking promontory, thin as its
Name and the hail flung off the skerry
We stop, breathless, laughing, looking
Round. We, the inheritors, looking round
To receive what we will never understand.
But beginning our occupation with faith.

# Rhigos

The cannon-smoke rolling
Off the Beacons engulfs the car.
The violence is over
Yet a promise of lightning
With its cordite tang hangs over
The khaki drab of Hirwaun.

Above this mist they gaze
From the stacked flats:
Faces between the turrets,
Hands clenched without weapons.
The only armour here
Is isolation that toughens

The mind, hardens eyes
That stare from siege. I think
Of the people who live
On these battlements: old
Women white and frail as moths,
The men mulattoed by alcohol,

Their frustration which burnt
A hole in life itself burnt out.
Leaving nothing. And as we grind
Over the mountain gridiron
I know they are seeking us
And our movement's illusion

Of freedom, those old people
Standing at their balconies
In the fresh wind, yet
Seeing instead this prow
Of Glamorgan — the black
And naked Rhigos, a whalebacked

Massif that supports
Nothing of their life, that
Is no comfort, yet is the earth
To which they are fused —
Its cloud and violet skeins of light;
An unendurable rock.

JOHN TRIPP

# In the National Museum

I went there on Tuesdays
at lunchtime, to look
at the Impressionists. Their colours
could take me into an old French summer
and let Cardiff sink in the Taff.
I never told her I went there
because she despised arty men.

Outside, at the top of the steps,
I took off my deerstalker
and hid my sandwich-tin behind a pillar.
Inside, under the big dome and high balcony,
there was dignity in the marble hush.
I adjusted my steel-rimmed specs
for the feast ahead. Then I saw the back of her
with an arm through some man's
going up the wide stairs. I turned back
to the revolving doors, scared,
thinking I would strangle her later.
She was wearing her best dress
and her hair was like flame.

## Eglwys Newydd

The village is straddled on both sides
of a main road. Sometimes it shakes
from heavy transport and rock blasting.
A shabby brook runs through it,
mossed blue slate and cheapjack granite
of functional dwellings, crumbling since Victoria.
The most terrible accent in Wales
ends here, and the authentic one begins a mile away
in Tongwynlais. The pubs are full of silence.
Oliver Cromwell spent a night in a house
that is now a greengrocer's.
                            It is one of those zones
for D.P.s between England and Wales,
a Gaza Strip where nobody belongs.
If you asked them how their search
for identity was getting on, they'd look blank
or say you needed certifying
in the asylum up the road.
                            It is one of the settlements
Rowland Lee would have praised,
being cleared of swarthy troublemakers
and neutered of Welshry. Dic Penderyn
would have yawned his head off.
                            Loyalty to the crown
hangs in pastry and sweet shops
where the ladies and gentlemen come
to open things. Controversy is swept with fag-ends
into the gutter.
                            I don't know why I live here.
I have been waiting a long time
for my visa to Tongwynlais.

# Capital

This will be the last ditch to fall
to the swing of its country.
Significance blowing down the hills
dies on the wind. Here the puffed
clink in their chains of office,
and the hagglers squat like a junta.

It is still as separate as an arm
lopped from its body: a strange sleeve
of territory spilled across the border.
What time has so carelessly mixed
clots here, where the ideals sag
and roots sprout only on the surface.

As long as I remember, the droll warmth
of its people has blurred
when our flag is lifted. Mouths are stitched.
Nothing is put to close scrutiny;
a knotted topic is flicked
into the bin, with a grin for Wales.

But now, in the distance, I think I hear
the young villagers build our future,
laying the first bricks of change.
This capital means less to them
than the land, where everything stems.
'Wait,' they are saying. 'Wait for us.'

# Penarth

When I was a runt, dragged
across its boring pebbles by my Bargoed
uncles, the Esplanade Hotel was full
of touring rugby packs, their names
hallowed in Playfair, boozing
like galleons awash in the long bar.
The upper velvet rooms were nests
for rich merchants and their doxies —
unclean weekends smeared on the clock
of their money pile-up. The wives
knew, accepted, and kept their peace.
Puritans spluttered at this citadel of sin.

Here were the tended bloombeds, the washed
war memorial, a neat tidy welcome
from this hamlet by the sea.
Our local spa, our small Baden-Baden
watering-place, it was quick down the Rhymney
Valley to that unsanded strip:
the wafers, cornets, fish-and-chips,
donkey rides on the cliff, and the hustling
Leica-snappers being so daft
as to corner our brood of colliers.
My plump aunt ran a teak-bodied Alvis,
closed, chauffeured and smooth,
fluttering her bloodshot eyes through the glass
as she paraded Penarth.

I go there now, a life later,
sipping dry Martini in the boat-club,
picking at chicken in the posh Caprice,
sure of nothing in the autumn chill —
almost hoping to see the young hookers
and the hucksters with their wiggling strumpets
enter again the crumbling Esplanade ...

# Scratch farmer

We argued. Running poor land had to be
about slick methods. I think his belief
was in the equal ration of sun and rainfall.
On a bog backholding behind some engine sheds
survival meant pigs, lean pork to compete.
Flop-hatted in dripping heat, he stooped to it.

He kept the sty as clean as a horse box;
a few geese fattened on corn in the orchard
where windfalls made head-blowing cider.
He remembered when the freight came through
and the overdug quarries were full of men,
when people bought pork with a peach-fed look.

The scratched patch reverted to dock and nettle.
A worn cog in the country wheel, tardily he creaked
into debt, sold his shack and pigs and geese.
At fifty he limped down to the rackety coast
to a caravan slum on the candyfloss strip
and stirred vats in a fish-and-chip trough.

# Epitaph at Gilfach Goch

I

Duffled against a knuckleduster wind
I crouch by the last rusted tram
tilted on a bank of tussock;
a drift of March snow
caps the eternal mountain;
two boys fly by on shag ponies
flicking their rope switches.
        Clear across the gap
like a skeleton of dead merriment
is the shell of the Six Bells.

This ripped hollow brings me back
as in some haunting — a tarted grave
where the well-meaning fumbled.
               There
the Britannic thundered, a frail thatch
of green lidding its scar;
under my boots lie the rich
thick districts of coal, now seamed forever.
Across the scoop, thin grass thrusts from slag
        above a fake waterfall,
rock culverts taming the stream
        of its old wildness.
Vandals in the boredom of static
struck at one eyeless chapel...
the high wheels and engine-sheds,
tramway and winding-house
gone for scrap...

## II

Men, in their blueprint wisdom
came here with explosive estimates,
heavy gear and miles of pipe;
slabs, brick, fence, saplings,
trucks of seed for the slopes
to sculpt a park from a battlefield,
to build a haven in the waste.
A dawn-to-dusk 'dozer fleet
moved the screen of black alps from the bed.

They worked for some just benevolence,
a soft canopy over the past;
errors of reckless men
would be corrected, the price of dust
atoned, proof of revival soon given
to a dead rut. 'See,' the slide-rulers said.
'Observe what we have done. We have mended
your devastated cup. It is a lovely
                  green Eden we have shaped.'

## III

Who dares jib at such noble motive
in this desolate garden they have left,
like a skull with bluebells in its sockets?
How could they know of the pumpless heart?
            The bustling past is locked
only in the memory of a dwindling few
mulled on vestiges of warmth;
they inherit a shuttered plot,
                        the commune of ghosts.
All that moneyed skill, the dream and wine
of the landscaper, ends here in a gutted void.
Severed pocket, once thriving to the rhythm
of its shifts, dies slowly on the soulless rim.
                  Beyond this rusted tram
and fleece-hung wire, tangled bramble in scrub —
beyond the broken, blasted, footworn moor
and the fox's home, there is only a Senghenydd
silence, and the old companion of wind
                  huddling its people...

# Soil

At the marbled institute
far from any wool-tufted rusty wire,
this brisk tutor in Rural Studies
    said farmers became farmers
    because they didn't like people.

No argument there. I could believe
the land-grubber's flint of hostility
in his vision of soft fools.
    I had just come from hard Cwmowen
on the uplands of Epynt —
so bleak remote,
their notion of a big night
was at Conti's café in Builth.

They clung like burrs to those bald slopes,
scraping till sunset, rising at dawn;
winter's early dusk was welcome.
No window framed a Constable
or a gentle watercolour.
                For them
it was a history of muck,
generations through a plod of clay —
unsentimental as ferrets
in their rattletraps by flickering tallow...

That mess, so close to the animal,
was what my worn-out grandad called
the disaster of agriculture:
a bad way to survive,
governed by the clock and too much weather,
that whittled his life away.

# A note from Plwmp

With a name like that
we had to stop. It conjured pictures
of fat friendly shopkeepers
and comfortable landladies, gossiping in Welsh.
True enough, they gave us bacon sandwiches
and tea for two florins.
Around the corner a student
hot from Aber was painting road-signs.

I looked at this piece of Wales —
old, hospitable, rebellious
still weaving the lingo on a taut loom
they kept to a bardic codicil
boxed and clean on the shelf of speech.
Down south it dropped like a fart
at Elizabeth's table, as strange as English
in Sebastopol. It cut like a lost lament
through the flat twang of merchants.

Only a gull's flight from Mersey
they stitch this lexicon,
laying new pages and mending the old.
That student had a brave new pluck:
he risked Judge Jeffreys and the cold assize,
the grey wigs who push a plainsong
back down the throat.

We left little Plwmp like pilgrims
who had just seen Jordan,
knowing the sea dawns would break
over the language of Cardigan.

# At Bosherston Ponds

In November it is desolate, and distant
from the ruck of summer. The mashed carpet of leaves
lie apple-rust in the grave-gaps,
their season done. Waves of high grass
wash about the church, drowning
the sunk mounds, the lopsided slabs
askew from weather and dying stock.
Names illegible beneath layered moss
clip me to futility, yet give that mild
pleasure we feel in cemeteries.
I am cousined to them by nothing
but a moment in Wales
and the loom of skulled union
under roof of turf with the winning maggot.
History on this dot of the map
is sufficient to make me limp
a foot high. In my pocket a poem
shrivels to pinpoint. I look backward
for the peglegs hobbling
while I walk in cold time. I slither down
a long path mucked to a whirl of dung
and hang onto branches for support.
                          Solitary now
on a balsa bridge across the lily ponds,
I lose all strut.
Skidding along slotted planks, the bridge shakes
as my flimsy tenure shakes. I look out
at sheer rock and sloped dune, stretches
of water lily: something perfect occurred here
long ago, hacked in silence
without men or words — gaunt-winter-perfect
in frame of steel...
                          I turn back
up the steep track of churned cattle mud
where dead anglers trod, full of their hooked skill,
and riders stumbled, chasing a streak of vermin.
                          I scramble up
to slap of sea wind in my face
howling through the lost cemetery.
To the bang of winter, the coming events
and the illusion of action.

GILLIAN CLARKE

# Letter from a Far Country

They have gone. The silence resettles
slowly as dust on the sunlit
surfaces of the furniture.
At first the skull itself makes
sounds in any fresh silence,
a big sea running in a shell.
I can hear my blood rise and fall.

Dear husbands, fathers, forefathers,
this is my apologia, my
letter home from the future,
my bottle in the sea which might
take a generation to arrive.

The morning's all activity.
I draw the detritus of a family's
loud life before me, a snow plough,
a road-sweeper with my cart of leaves.
The washing machine drones
in the distance. From time to time
as it falls silent I fill baskets
with damp clothes and carry them
into the garden, hang them out,
stand back, take pleasure counting
and listing what I have done.
The furniture is brisk with polish.
On the shelves in all of the rooms
I arrange the books
in alphabetical order
according to subject: Mozart,
Advanced Calculus, William,
and Paddington Bear.
Into the drawers I place your clean
clothes, pyjamas with buttons
sewn back on, shirts stacked neatly
under their labels on the shelves.
The chests and cupboards are full,
the house sweet as a honeycomb.
I move in and out of the hive
all day, harvesting, ordering.
You will find all in its proper place,
When I have gone.

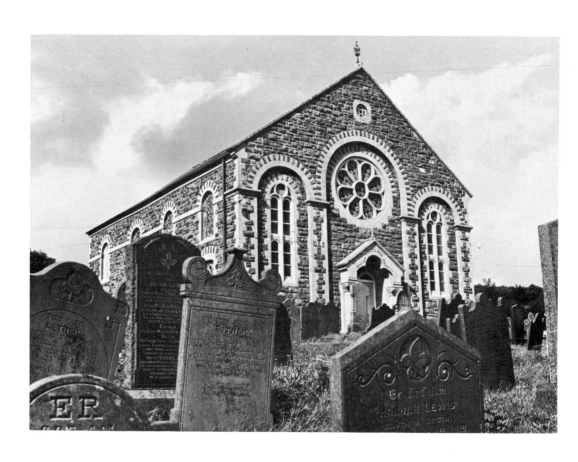

As I write I am far away.
First see a landscape. Hill country,
essentially feminine,
the sea not far off. Its blues
widen the sky. Bryn Isaf
down there in the crook of the hill
under Calfaria's single eye.
My grandmother might have lived there.
Any farm. Any chapel.
Father and minister, on guard,
close the white gates to hold her.
A stony track turns between
ancient hedges, narrowing,
like a lane in a child's book.
Its perspective makes the heart restless
like the boy in the rhyme, his stick
and cotton bundle on his shoulder.

The minstrel boy to the war has gone.
But the girl stays. To mind things.
She must keep. And wait. And pass time.

There's always been time on our hands.
We read this perfectly white page
for the black head of the seal,
for the cormorant, as suddenly gone
as a question from the mind,
snaking underneath the surfaces.
A cross of gull shadow on the sea
as if someone stepped on its grave.
After an immeasurable space
the cormorant breaks the surface
as a small, black, returning doubt.

From here the valley is narrow,
the lane lodged like a halfway ledge.
From the opposite wood the birds
ring like a tambourine. It's not
the birdsong of a garden, thrush
and blackbird, robin and finch,
distinguishable, taking turn.

The song's lost in saps and seepings,
amplified by hollow trees,
cupped leaves and wind in the branches.
All their old conversations
collected carefully, faded
and difficult to read, yet held
forever as voices in a well.

Reflections and falling stones; shouts
into the scared dark of lead-mines;
the ruined warehouse where the owls stare;
sea-caves; cellars; the back stairs
behind the chenille curtain;
the landing when the lights are out;
nightmares in hot feather beds;
the barn where I'm sent to fetch Taid;
that place where the Mellte flows
boldly into limestone caves
and leaps from its hole a mile on,
the nightmare still wild in its voice.

When I was a child a young boy
was drawn into a pipe and drowned
at the swimming pool. I never
forgot him, and pity rivers
inside mountains, and the children
of Hamelin sucked in by music.
You can hear children crying
from the empty woods.
It's all given back in concert
with the birds and leaves and water
and the song and dance of the Piper.

Listen! to the starlings glistening
on a March morning! Just one day
after snow, an hour after frost,
the thickening grass begins to shine
already in the opening light.
There's wind to rustle the blood,
the sudden flame of crocus.

My grandmother might be standing
in the great silence before the Wars.
Hanging the washing between trees
over the white and the red hens.
Sheets, threadworked pillowcases.
Mamgu's best pais, her Sunday frock.

The sea stirs restlessly between
the sweetness of clean sheets,
the lifted arms,
the rustling petticoats.

My mother's laundry list, ready
on Mondays when the van called.
The rest soaked in glutinous starch
and whitened with a bluebag
kept in a broken cup.

(In the airing cupboard you'll see
a map, numbering and placing
every towel, every sheet.
I have charted all your needs.)

It has always been a matter
of lists. We have been counting,
folding, measuring, making,
tenderly laundering cloth
ever since we have been women.

The waves are folded meticulously,
perfectly white. Then they are tunbled
and must come to be folded again.

Four herring gulls and their shadows
are shouting at the clear glass
of a shaken wave. The sea's a sheet
bellying in the wind, snapping.
Air and white linen. Our airing cupboards
are full of our satisfactions.

The gulls grieve at our contentment.
It is a masculine question.
'Where' they call 'are your great works?'
They slip their fetters and fly up
to laugh at land-locked women.
Their cries are cruel as greedy babies.

Our milky tendernesses dry
to crisp lists; immaculate
linen; jars labelled and glossy
with our perfect preserves.
Spiced oranges; green tomato
chutney; seville orange marmalade
annually staining gold
the snows of January

(the saucers of marmalade
are set when the amber wrinkles
like the sea if you blow it)

Jams and jellies of blackberry,
crabapple, strawberry, plum,
greengage and loganberry.
You can see the fruit pressing
their little faces against the glass;
tiny onions imprisoned
in their preservative juices.

Familiar days are stored whole
in bottles. There's a wet morning
orchard in the dandelion wine;
a white spring distilled
in elderflower's clarity;
and a loving, late, sunburning
day of October in syrups
of rose hip and the beautiful
black sloes that stained the gin to rose.

It is easy to make of love
these ceremonials. As priests
we fold cloth, break bread, share wine,
hope there's enough to go round.

(You'll find my inventories pinned
inside all of the cupboard doors.)

Soon they'll be planting the barley.
I imagine I see it, stirring
like blown sand, feel the stubble
cutting my legs above blancoed
daps in a summer too hot
for Wellingtons. The cans of tea
swing squeakily on wire loops,
outheld, not to scald myself,
over the ten slow leagues
of the field of golden knives.
To be out with the men, at work,
I had longed to carry their tea,
for the feminine privilege,
for the male right to the field.
Even that small task made me bleed.
Halfway between the flowered lap
of my grandmother and the black
heraldic silhouette of men
and machines on the golden field,
I stood crying, my ankle bones
raw and bleeding like the poppies
trussed in the corn stooks in their torn
red silks and soft mascara blacks.

(The recipe for my best bread,
half granary meal, half strong brown flour,
water, sugar, yeast and salt,
is copied out in the small black book)

In the black book of this parish
a hundred years ago
you will find the unsupported
woman had 'pauper' against her name.
She shared it with old men.

The parish was rich with movement.
The woollen mills were spinning.
Water-wheels milled the sunlight
and the loom's knock was a heart
behind all activity.
The shuttles were quick as birds
in the warp of the oakwoods.
In the fields the knives were out
in a glint of husbandry.
In back bedrooms, barns and hedges,
in hollows of the hills,
the numerous young were born.

The people were at work:
dressmaker; wool carder; quilter;
midwife; farmer; apprentice;
house servant; scholar; labourer;
shepherd; stocking knitter; tailor;
carpenter; mariner; ploughman;
wool spinner; cobbler; cottager;
Independent Minister.

And the paupers: Enoch Elias
and Ann, his wife; David Jones,
Sarah and Esther their daughter;
Mary Evans and Ann Tanrallt;
Annie Cwm March and child;
Eleanor Thomas, widow, Cryg Glas;
Sara Jones, 84, and daughter;
Nicholas Rees, aged 80, and his wife;
Mariah Evans the Cwm, widow;
on the parish for want of work.
Housebound by infirmity, age,
widowhood, or motherhood.
Before the Welfare State who cared
for sparrows in a hard spring?

The stream's cleaner now; it idles
past derelict mill-wheels; the drains
do its work. Since the tanker sank
the unfolding rose of the sea

blooms on the beaches, wave on wave
black, track-marked, each tide
a procession of the dead.
Slack water's treacherous; each veined
wave is a stain in seal-milk;
the sea gapes, hopelessly
licking itself.

(Examine
your hands scrupulously
for signs of dirt in your own blood.
And wash them before meals.)

In that innocent smallholding
where the swallows live and field mice
winter and the sheep barge in
under the browbone, the windows
are blind, are doors for owls,
bolt-holes for dreams. The thoughts have flown.
The last death was a suicide.
The lowing cows discovered her,
the passing bell of their need
warned a winter morning that day
when no one came to milk them.
Later, they told me, a baby
was born in the room where she died,
as if by this means sanctified,
a death outcried by a birth.
Middle-aged, poor, isolated,
she could not recover
from mourning an old parent's death.
Influenza brought an hour
too black, too narrow to escape.

More mysterious to them
was the woman who had everything.
A village house with railings;
rooms of good furniture;
fine linen in the drawers;
a garden full of herbs and flowers;
a husband in work; grown sons.

She had a cloud on her mind,
they said, and her death shadowed them.
It couldn't be explained.
I watch for her face looking out,
small and white, from every window,
like a face in a jar. Gossip,
whispers, lowing sounds. Laughter.

The people have always talked.
The landscape collects conversations
as carefully as a bucket,
gives them back in concert
with a wood of birdsong.

(If you hear your name in that talk
don't listen. Eavesdroppers never
heard anything good of themselves.)

When least expected you catch
the eye of the enemy
looking coldly from the old world.
Here's a woman who ought to be
up to her wrists in marriage;
not content with the second hand
she is shaking the bracelets
from her hands. The sea circles
her ankles. Watch its knots loosen
from the delicate bones
of her feet, from the rope of foam
about a rock. The seal swims
in a collar of water
drawing the horizon in its wake.
And doubt breaks the perfect
white surface of the day.

About the tree in the middle
of the cornfield the loop of gold
is loose as water; as the love
we should bear one another.

When I rock the sea rocks. The moon
doesn't seem to be listening
invisible in a pale sky,
keeping a light hand on the rein.
Where is woman in this trinity?
The mare who draws the load?
The hand on the leather?
The cargo of wheat?
Watching sea-roads I feel
the tightening white currents,
am waterlogged, my time set
by the sea's town clock.
My cramps and drownings, energies,
desires draw the loaded net
of the tide over the stones.

A lap full of pebbles and then
light as a Coca Cola can.
I am freight. I am ship.
I cast ballast overboard.
The moon decides my Equinox.
At high tide I am leaving.

The women are leaving.
They are paying their taxes
and dues. Filling in their passports.
They are paying to Caesar
what is Caesar's, to God what is God's.
To woman what is Man's.

I hear the dead grandmothers,
Mamgu from Ceredigion,
Nain from the North, all calling
their daughters down from the fields,
calling me in from the road.
They haul at the taut silk cords;
set us fetching eggs, feeding hens,
mixing rage with the family bread,
lock us to the elbows in soap suds.
Their sculleries and kitchens fill
with steam, sweetnesses, goosefeathers.

On the graves of my grandfathers
the stones, in their lichens and mosses,
record each one's importance.
Diaconydd. Trysorydd.
Pillars of their society.
Three times at chapel on Sundays.
They are in league with the moon
but as silently stony
as the simple names of their women.

We are hawks trained to return
to the lure from the circle's
far circumference. Children sing
that note that only we can hear.
The baby breaks the waters,
disorders the blood's tune, sets
each filament of the senses
wild. Its cry tugs at flesh, floods
its mother's milky fields.
Nightly in white moonlight I wake
from sleep one whole slow minute
before the hungry child
wondering what woke me.

School's out. The clocks strike four.
Today this letter goes unsigned,
unfinished, unposted.
When it is finished
I will post it from a far country.

# The Water Diviner

His fingers tell water like prayer.
He hears its voice in the silence
through fifty feet of rock
on an afternoon still with drought.

Under an old tin bath, a stone,
an upturned can, his copper pipe
glints with discovery. We dip our hose
deep into the dark, sucking its dryness,

till suddenly the water answers,
not the little sound we know,
but a thorough bass too deep
for the naked ear, shouts through the hose

a word we could not say, or spell, or remember,
something like 'Dŵr...dŵr'.

# Buzzard

No sutures in the steep brow
of this cranium, as in mine
or yours. Delicate ellipse
as smooth as her own egg

or the cleft flesh of a fruit.
From the plundered bones on the hill,
like a fire in its morning ashes,
you guess it's a buzzard's skull.

You carry it gently home,
hoping no Last Day of the birds
will demand assembly
of her numerous white parts.

In the spaces we can't see
on the other side of walls
as fine as paper, brain and eye
dry out under the gossamers.

Between the sky and the mouse
that moves at the barley field's
spinning perimeter, only
a mile of air and the ganging

crows, their cries stones at her head.
In death, the last stoop, all's risked.
She scorns the scavengers
who feed on death, and never

feel the lightning flash of heart
dropping on heart, warm fur, blood.

# East Moors

At the end of a bitter April
the cherries flower at last in Penylan.
We notice the white trees and the flash
of sea with two blue islands beyond
the city, where the steelworks used to smoke.

I live in the house I was born in,
am accustomed to the sudden glow
of flame in the night sky, the dark sound
of something heavy dropped, miles off,
the smell of sulphur almost natural.

In Roath and Rumney now, washing strung
down the narrow gardens will stay clean.
Lethargy settles in front rooms and wives
have lined up little jobs for men to do.

A few men stay to see it through. Theirs
the bitterest time as rolling mills
make rubble. Demolition gangs
erase skylines whose hieroglyphs
recorded all our stories.

I am reminded of that Sunday
years ago when we brought the children
to watch two water cooling towers
blown up, recall the appalling void
in the sunlight, like a death.

On this first day of May an icy
rain is blowing through this town,
quieter, cleaner, poorer from today.
The cherries are in flower in Penylan.
Already over East Moors the sky whitens, blind.

JEREMY HOOKER

# Hill country rhythms

Sometimes I glimpse a rhythm
I am not part of, and those who are
could never see.
    The hawk I disturb
at his kill, leaving bodiless,
bloody wings spread, curves
away and with a sharp turn
follows the fence; and the fence
lining a rounded bank flies
smoothly downhill, then rises
to wind-bowed trees whose shape
the clouds take on, and the ridge
running under them, where
the sky bears round in a curve.
On the mountainside stands
a square white farm, its roof
a cutting edge, but it too
moves with shadow and cloud.
    I glimpse this
with the hawk in view, lose it
to fenceposts and trees holding
a still day down, and wings
dismembered at my feet, while
down the road comes a neighbour
singing loudly, with his herd
big-uddered, slowly swaying.

# Beidog

Sunlight and shallow water,
rock, stones with red marks
like cuts of a rusty axe,
dark under hazel and alder,
broken white on blackened steps
and below the falls a cold pale green —
how shall I celebrate this,
    always present
under our sleep and thoughts,
where we do not see ourselves
    reflected
or know the language of memory
gathered from its fall?

Beidog running dark
    between us
and our neighbours, down
from Mynydd Bach —
this is the stream I wish to praise
    and the small mountain.

I am not of you, tongue
through whom Taliesin descends the ages
gifted with praise, who know
that praise turns dust to light.
    In my tongue,
of all arts
this is the most difficult.

# Brynbeidog

For ten years the sycamores
have turned about us, the Beidog
has run with leaves, and ice and sun.
I have turned the earth, thrown up
blue chip and horseshoe; from near fields
sheep and bullocks have looked in.

We have shared weathers
with the stone house; kept its silence;
listened under winds lifting slates
for a child's cry; all we have
the given space has shaped, pointing
our lights seen far off
as a spark among scattered sparks.
      The mountain above
has been rock to my drifting mind.

Where all is familiar, around us
the country with its language
gives all things other names;
there is darkness on bright days
and on the stillest a wind
that will not let us settle,
but blows the dust from loved
things not possessed or known.

# The mason's law

Though the slate
where his hand slipped
could not stand
    worthy of a name,
at least it could lie
in his living room,
set in the floor.

*Er Cof* unfinished,
under our feet, recalls
the mason and his law:
    Honour the dead
with your craft;
waste nothing; leave
no botched memorial.

# Wind blew once

Wind blew once till it seemed
the earth would be skinned from the fields,
the hard roots bared.
      Then it was again
a quiet October,
red berries on grey rock
and blue sky, with a buzzard crying.

I scythed half-moons in long grass,
with nettle-burn stinging my arms,
bringing the blood's rhythm back.
      At night
in our room we lay in an angle
between two streams,
with sounds of water meeting,
      and by day
the roads ran farther,
joined and formed a pattern
at the edge of vast, cloudy hills.

      The house was small
against the mountain; from above,
a stone on a steep broad step
of falling fields; but around us
the walls formed a deep channel,
with marks of other lives, holding
its way from worked moorland
to this Autumn with an open sky.

# Common land above Trefenter

This is no haunt
For the painter of prospects.

Sheep will not bleat a complaint
Or the barn owl hoot derision,
Where poverty abounded
Providing shelter.

On bared common, where
Nocturnal migrants homed,
There is room for the kite
Cleaned out of cities, none
For the import of terror,

For alien shadow
In common daylight,
Or fashion
Of nightmare or grandeur:

Thin cawl
On the valley's bread line
Is not its provider, nor
Dwellings built in a night,
Fields wide as an axe throw
From the door, patterning
Moorland with stony patches.

Only the bare history
Under foot — holdings

Untenable, falling back
Into quarries: last post
Of hedge-bank craftsmen,
With breast plough and mattock,
On the road to the coalface.

# Shepherd

Others have died or left;
he has grown louder, bigger,
filling the fields which he keeps
with an old skill.

I picture him through glass,
framed in the window,
against the mountain:

tall, strongly made,
ruddy from wind and sun,
a man who strides, sings,
waves a stick, then shouts
at his dogs with a voice
they will hear in the village.

And he turns, walks
through the frame, as he has
since he came as a boy
and stood with his father
saying aye, aye...

## As a thousand years

Not a soul, only
a stubble field, bales
like megaliths; a flight
of trees over the Beidog,
and behind, darker green,
at the back of the sky,
the ridge damming
the sun; then,
      for a breath,
there was no sign of us.
Not a soul, only
light flooding this field,
bright as a marigold.

## Leaving

Against the wall
a boy's bike leans
waiting for its rider.

I look from the stream
through a sycamore —
breakfast things on the table
wait in place;
vapour trails shine
like ruts in the sky
on airways far to the south.

Sun on the ridge.
The house filled with light.

*For the first time*
*it is hollow, echoing,*
*the living room*
*cavernous.*

As I walk away
the Beidog winds, gleaming —
joining field to field.

I climb and the sea rises,
silver, a planet's rim;
peak climbs on peak,
blue and far,

the house settles —
smaller, deeper, in place.

*Do we simply*
   *pack ourselves away?*
*The hearth's a black hole*
*where you knelt.*

After days of storm,
fallen slates, fields
grey with exhaustion,
buzzards come, and a kite
picking red slivers,

a ewe shelters lambs
at the lattice of a thorn.

*Floors skinned,*
*picture shapes on walls,*
*in each doorway*
*a shock of cold.*

Under hills clouded,
bent backed,

I crumble black earth
through fingers
caked with earth:

ground worked
over and over, where
we too grow round
with windbreak sycamores.

> *Just now*
> *I put out my hand*
> *for a table, which this morning*
> *I broke up and burnt*
>
> *and nearly fell,*
> *nearly leant on its rim.*

Midsummer silence falls,
the dry lanes smell
of dog roses and dust.

Foxgloves snake from hedgerows,
a buzzard circles mewing
round and round.

I lie down,
dash the stream in my face,
look up at the slate roof
tilted against the ridge.

> *Bare, flesh coloured boards.*
> *Briefly*
> *in childless quiet*
> *the house waits.*

NIGEL JENKINS

# Maidenhair

The fern was all I wanted there;
the richer pickings — her lustre jugs,
the family dresser — were spoil I left
for other tastes. Grandpa's fern,
that dwelt with her, dwells now
with me, a mist of light
on the dark shelf.

Have I the touch, the
whispered skills, to bring it
after so hard a season
to its old brilliance?

I breathe *fern*, and say ancient,
link with primal trees
and the forests of heat locked up
in coal. I say *grandpa's fern*

and she who taught me
the naming of this and many things
opens a door
to rooms of sunlight and polish and fruit.
There sometimes we've found him, clouded
in smoke, a froth of ale beading
on his walrus moustache,
as he fumes against
progress, the workers and his gout.

They are dead, and their story.
There were things
I'd meant to ask: when to cut back?
what if, say, something —
a bullet perhaps — were to smash
its jar... how then to
re-pot — with leafmould or peat?

The maidenhair endures in the Celtic west.
Theirs they kept whole lifetimes
in the same narrow pot.
I'll give it space, learn its ways; help it
flourish, reproduce, watch me go.

# First calving

Up through the rain I'd driven her, taut
hocks out-sharing a streak of the caul,
and that single hoof, pale as lard,
poked out beneath her tail.

In shelter,
across the yard from me now,
her rump's whiteness fretted the dark.
I watched there the obscure passage
of men's hands and, exiled in crass
daylight, waited —
                                    till a shout
sent me running big with purpose
to the stable for a halter.

They flipped to me the rope's end, its
webbing they noosed around the hoof:
we leaned there, two of us, lending weight
to each contraction; the other fumbled
for the drowning muzzle, the absent leg,
        said he'd heard that over Betws way
                some farmer'd done this with a tractor —
                        pulled the calf to bits and killed the cow.

Again she pushed, and to first air
we brought the nostrils free; next the head
and blockaging shoulders, then out
he flopped, lay there like some bones pudding
steaming with life.

                Later,
she cleansed. I grubbed a hole in the earth
and carried the afterbirth out
on a shovel: to be weighted with a stone,
they said, to keep it from the scavengers.

# The ridger

Capsized, by some nosing cow,
in the headland where last unhitched,
it raises to the solitudes
guide-arm, wing and wheel.

What should slide or spin
locks to the touch; a bolt-head
flakes like mud-slate at the push
of a thumb — fit for the scrapyard
or, prettified with roses, some
suburban lawn. Yet there persist,
in a tuck away from the weather,
pinheads of blue original paint.

To describe is to listen, to enter
into detail with this ground
and this ground's labour; to take
and offer outward continuing fruit.

My palm smoothes the imperfect chill
of rusted iron... I weigh against
the free arm, easing up
the underside share — worms retire,
lice waggle away: it stands
on righted beam, rags of root-lace
draped from the delivered haft.

Maker and middleman emblazon
two cracked plaques: Ransomes, Ipswich;
White Bros., Pontardulais.
Less patent is the deeper tale
that gathers with the touch of rain
on the spike which was a handle,
the nail bent over for an axle-pin.

# Snowdrops

I know what I am doing here,

come every year
in the iron first month

to seek them out.

I choose my time,
a day to freeze
the waters of the eye,
and I move through it

— primal caver delving in sign —

to link with light
of the living blood.

* * * *

Last year too soon,

not a white word
in all the wood's deadness.

Home then speechless

to wait.

* * * *

Sky grey and lowering
curtains the wood:

no money, no food: hush
of alone here, cold
of hunger,

last place of warmth
a hole in the head
that's known, I remember, as mouth.

* * * *

A man in a coat
hunting flowers.

Sudden scatty cackle —
the waving of a branch:
a magpie, I trust, has left the tree.

Here, now
the blue gift amazing
of kingfisher flight

would not be believed.
I ask only

snowdrops,
A warmer world.

* * * *

And here they nod
in the cold and quiet.

*In Bolivia the soldiers*
*broke glass on the ground.*
*They made the naked children*
*lie flat on the glass,*
*they made the mothers walk*
*on the children's backs.*

Here snowdrops nod
in the quiet and cold.

*If the bomb fell on Swansea,*
*fifty miles away in Cardiff*
*eyeballs would melt...*

Can
        a flower?
Can
        the poem?

* * * *

Brother dead in Paviland:

the first I pick
I pick in celebration

of the species that stayed
when all others fled
the coming of the cold,

species now trembling
through a darker season
of its own manufacture.

* * * *

Feet gone dead, hand around the stems
some borrowed thing, a clamp
of frozen meat

but

tlws yr eira

blodyn yr eira

cloch maban

eirlys

lili wen fach

— a song in my fist.

* * * *

The owl is with her
the day's length,
and she is sick
of the moon:

her winters are long.

I hand her snowdrops:
she grasps the primrose.

* * * *

Inside from the cold
they boast no bouquet,

just green breath
of the earth's first things.

I find them a glass,
and on the worktable
scattered with papers
I place them.

It is enough.

* * * *

Thin sun creeps
upon the afternoon

and the water warms,
bubbles sprout
on the earthpale stems.

They'll die early, yes,
and drop no seed:

the year may live.

# Goat's Hole, Paviland

When bronze lay dreaming, and the ice
hoarded oceans at nearby north,
this huge vulva, aloof in the rock
to sea's thrust or man's, was home
to the hunter, his forge and grave.

Long wise to death, they
offered him outward with skull
of mammoth, lyric shells — charms
that so beguiled his finders
they thought they'd unearthed a woman.

In words of flint, in the dark
language of his own ruddled bones
the silt whispers news of his world:

a phrase of worked ivory outlines
an arm; your thumb's fit
with a dimpled stone sounds the voice
of trails, great voice of the herds
that were tidal here an age before
seas had discovered their plain.
Charred bones light a fire, speak
warm in-comings from the tundral cold —

to leap of shadow, meat-smoke
and the endless skill of fingers.

We piece back the pieces.

Though more than we have held
is hidden here, we, who have trailed
among the stars, are pleased to remember
what the earth has forgotten: furs
and baskets and tools of wood, the skull
of the man, his intelligence:

it's this softer thing — finer
than a flint's edge, tougher than stone —
that fashions amazement, keeps us guessing.

## Castell Carreg Cennen

Castell Carreg Cennen: helmet wrought
from the crag's limestone
to glower on Deheubarth: the brain
flown, twisting now in hideous freedom
to western sun & the strip at Brawdy.

To stand under shadow:
of stone's relentless sophistication, the word
Nagasaki: & no sudden white bird
on the darkening below
nor the sun's choosing of the faces of farms
can draw the soul from its coldness.

Today's invaders, a busload from Swansea,
their grey heads and hats like hydrangeas
lost in thistle, found among fern
as they straggle to the top.
. . . *& every Wednesday, the mystery voice* . . .
broody talk — of radio routines,
of cakes & curtains &
letters home from daughters & sons —
counterpoints description
of improved methods of waging war,
counterpoints rattle of the single cup
in the houseful of rooms.

. . . *the mystery voice, at 8.55 & again*
*at twenty-five minutes past nine* . . .

fresh eggs for sale in the farm below; they
linger, buying, & as we head for the bus
one of them hands me a clutch
of three — though what she says
there's no hearing, language
robbed from her mouth by a screaming jet.

Three fresh eggs:
warm in my palm long after the fighter
has rumbled into silence
through the arming skies.

# Land of song

(i.m. 1/3/79)

Oggy! Oggy! Oggy!
This is the music
of the Welsh machine
programmed — Oggy! — to sing
non-stop, and to think only
what it thinks it thinks
when it thinks in fact nothing.

Sing on, machine, sing
in your gents-only bar —
you need not budge an inch
to vanquish the foe,
to ravish again
the whore of your dreams,
to walk songful and proud
through the oggy oggy toyland
of Oggy Oggy Og.

Sing with the blinding hwyl
of it all: you are programmed
to sing: England expects —
*my hen laid a haddock*
and all that stuff.

Ar hyd y nos, ar hyd
y dydd — the songs, the songs,
the hymns and bloody arias
that churn from its mouth
like puked-up S.A. —
and not a word meant
not a word understood
by the Welsh machine.

Oggy! Oggy! Oggy!
shame dressed as pride.
The thing's all mouth,
needs a generous boot
up its oggy oggy arse
before we're all of us sung
into oggy oggy silence.

ANNE STEVENSON

# Himalayan Balsam

Orchid-lipped, loose-jointed, purplish, indolent flowers,
with a ripe smell of peaches, like a girl's breath through lipstick,
delicate and coarse in the weedlap of late summer rivers,
dishevelled, weak-stemmed, common as brambles, as love which

subtracts us from seasons, their courtships and murders,
(*Meta segmentata* in her web, and the male waiting,
between blossom and violent blossom, meticulous spiders
repeated in gossamer, and the slim males waiting...)

Fragrance too rich for keeping, too light to remember,
like grief for the cat's sparrow and the wild gull's
beach-hatched embryo. (She ran from the reaching water
with the broken egg in her hand, but the clamped bill

refused brandy and grubs, a shred too naked and perilous for
life offered freely in cardboard boxes, little windowsill
coffins for bird death, kitten death, squirrel death, summer
repeated and ended in heartbreak, in the sad small funerals.)

Sometimes, shaping bread or scraping potatoes for supper,
I have stood in the kitchen, transfixed by what I'd call love
if love were a whiff, a wanting for no particular lover,
no child, or baby or creature. 'Love, dear love'

I could cry to these scent-spilling ragged flowers
and mean nothing but'no', by that word's breadth,
to their evident going, their important descent through red towering
stalks to the riverbed. It's not, as I thought, that death

creates love. More that love knows death. Therefore
tears, therefore poems, therefore the long stone sobs of cathredrals
that speak to no ferret or fox, that prevent no massacre.
(I am combing abundant leaves from these icy shallows.)

Love, it was you who said, 'Murder the killer
we have to call life and we'd be a bare planet under a dead sun.'
Then I loved you with the usual soft lust of October
that says 'yes' to the coming winter and a summoning odour of balsam.

# Walking Early by the Wye

Through dawn in February's wincing radiance.
Every splinter of river mist
rayed in my eyes.

As if the squint of the sun had released light's
metals. As if the river pulsed white,
and the holly's

sharp green lacquered leaves leaped acetylene.
As if the air smouldered from the ice of dry
pain, as if day

were fragmented in doubt. As if it were given
to enter alive the braided rings Saturn
is known by

and yet be allied to the dyke's heaped mud.
I will not forget how the ash trees stood,
silvered and still,

how each soft stone on its near shadow knelt,
how the sheep became stones where they built
their pearled hill.

# Burnished

Walking out of Hay in the rain, imagining Blake
imagining the real world into existence,
I suddenly turned on him and said with energy —
How dare you inflict imagination on us!
What halo does the world deserve? And he —
Let worlds die burnished, as along this bank.

Beautiful, I said to him and to the world's brown
oiled by the cloud still wet in its spiny shell.
A gloss of red horses' flank shone in its name.
To hold, it was a smooth pebble
mountain water had been running over. Sculpted round,
it swam like an embryo in my palm.

Now close your eyes. I felt the whole world warmed.
It was breathing its native heat in my blind skin.
When I looked again, it was a leather ocean
lapping a small sandy island. No one
appeared to live there. Now where its gleam had been
is a breast with a shrivelled nipple, like a dry wound.

# Green Mountain, Black Mountain

I

White pine, sifter of sunlight,
Wintering host in New England woods,
Cold scent, icicle to the nostril,
Path without echo, unmarked page.

> I formed you, you forget me,
> I keep you like a fossil.
> The air is full of footprints.
> Rings of the sycamore spell you.
> Your name spills out on April ground
>            with October leafmould...

Beechbole, cheekbone of the interior,
Sugaring maple, tap of sour soil,
Woody sweetness, wine of the honeybark,
Mountain trickle, bitter to the tongue.

> You acquired me out of wilderness,
> Grey maples streaked with birches,
> With your black-shuttered
> White wooden houses flanked with porches,
> Your black-painted peeling front doors.

Pairs of shuttered windows,
Sheltered lives.
Child's work, the symmetry,
Thin graves for narrow souls.

> Terra there was before *Terra Nova*.
> You brought to my furred hills
> Axes, steeples; your race split
> Hugely on the heave of the Atlantic...

In April the earth serves patiently its purpose.
Trees unclench their closed crimson fists
Against return. How many weeks before ease will annul
These dark, matted, snow-beaten scraps of mowin?

Dry wind-eaten beechleaves
Flutter under their birth arch.
Steeplebush and blackberry
Stoop to beginnings.

Green mountain with its shadow future,
Unwritten days in the buried stone.
Black mountain, colour of roots,
Clay in the roof, gag to the mouth.

II

In border Powys, a landrover
stalls on a hilltrack.
A farmer gets out with a halter,
plods to a sodden field where
a mare and her colt have rolled
the wet soil of Welsh weather
all a mud-lashed winter.

Unlatching the gate, he
forces the halter on the caked
anxious head of the mare,
then leads her away to where
a plan of his own makes fast
to some spindle purpose
the fate of the three of them.

The inscrutable movements of the man
puzzle the horses, who
follow him, nevertheless,
up the piebald track,
snowdeep in drift in places,
tyre-churned with red mud.

These are the Black Mountains
where the drenched sleep of Wales
troubles King Arthur in his cave,
where invisible hankerings of the dead
trouble the farms spilled over them —
the heaped fields, graves and tales.

And he, with his brace of horses,
barker at strangers, inbreeder of races,
is Teyrnon still, or Pryderi the colt-child,
fixed without shape or time
between the ghost-pull of Annwfn —
that other world, underworld, feathering
green Wales in its word-mist —

And the animal pull of his green dunged boots,
which take him, as he takes his horses,
up a red and white track for which he has
no name. A habit. An inheritance.
A cold night's work getting lambs born.
And in the morning, again.

III

Rain in the wind
        and the green need of again
                opening in this Welsh woods.

'Vermont' I want to call it,
        'Green Mountain', rafter
                over sleepers in the black

hill of returnings, shadows
        in the dry cave
                of the happened.

At a peal of memory
        they rise in tatters, imperatives,
                the word fossils,

webs of thready handwriting,
        typewritten strata, uncut stones
                culled for the typesetters' cemeteries.

*

If you, mother, had survived
        you would have written...

As when we were children
        and everything was going on
                forever in New Haven

you scratched in your journal —
        *It is a strange reaction but*
        *suddenly the war has made it*
        *imperative to spend time at home*
        *reading and being with my children.*

The pen drew its meanings
        through vacancy,
                threading a history.

*

And what shall I do
        with this touchable page that has
                closed over doubt in her voice these forty years?

I set the words up on the table,
        feeling for continuities,
                tap them with my quick nail. Listen.

But her shell has buried her echo in them.
        It is small, hard, a child's tooth,
                a guilt-pebble, a time preserved like an ammonite.

Then maybe on the second
        or the third day of March
                you overhear a blackbird in a dead elm,

or a thrush singing almost before you wake,
    or you walk unexpectedly into the calm
        ravage of a riverbank

where a broken branch
    kneels into rising water to remake
        predictable green tips,

and I know that it matters
    and does not matter —
        it is you in me who lives these things.

*

We'd thought she'd want us, knowing it was cancer,
But when we went to her she winced.
Her hand became a supplicating blur
That winter, and we didn't see her much.
There was a kind of wilting away in her
As if she couldn't bear the human touch
Of voices. Or was it something more
Unkind in us... resentful helplessness,
A guilty anger. She was dying
At us. Dying was accusing.

IV

After April snow,
such a green thaw.
A chiff-chaff chips a warmer home
in that cloud-cliff.
The river bulges,
flexing brown Japanese muscles,
moving its smooth planes in multitudes.
Threads of white melt stitch
the slashed flanks of the hill fields.

Soon the animal will be well again,
hunting and breeding
in grass-covered bones.
It peers from these clinical windows
apprehensive but healing.
To be whole would be enough.
To be whole and well and warm,
content with a kill.

V

Crossing the Atlantic. That child-pure
    impulse of away, retreating
        to our God-forgetting present

from the God-rot of old Boston and Leyden.
    'To remove to some other place
        for sundry weighty and solid reasons.'

And then to be the letter of the place,
    the page of the Lord's approval, within
        the raw green misery of the risk.

'For there they shall be liable to
    famine and nakedness
        and the want, in a manner, of all things.'

Without things, then, the thing was to be done,
    the mountain changed, the chance
        regiven. Taken again.

*

Crossing the Atlantic. Passport,
    briefcase, two trays full of cellophane food
        and a B grade film.

No, father, I mean
    across to the America
        that lives in the film of my mind.

You would have to be
    alive there, distilled
        on the spool of your life,

not as a photograph —
    unhappiness or happiness staring
        from the onceness of a time —

but as the living practice of a now,
    rehearsed as certain habits and expressions —
        your shoulders' loosened stoop to the piano,

or the length of you decanted on a chair,
        animate in argument, ash scattered
                from your cigarette like punctuation.

I think of the goodness of the house,
        the companionable presences of cellos
                punished in the corners like children,

or gleaming like the muscle-backs of girls,
        smug in the enslavement of one lover
                or another since the eighteenth century

made its music bread and water
        for the likes of us who,
                having no other faith,

still kept our covenant with
        foreign Bach, with Schubert,
                after-dinner Mozart, Razumovskis...

(The Polish ghettos
        drained into the cattle cars.
                Dying Vienna bled us violins.)

And yet through those
        immortal-seeming summers,
                music, that rare mediant window,

was glass through which we grew,
        a grace we had not
                guilt enough to refuse.

*

Chestnut blossom with its crimson stigmata,
Stamen-thrust from confused hands —
Five white petals, multiple in a
Competing order, so that each candlelabrum stands
As a tree of defeats around a *pietà*...

To be as one mother in a storm of sons,
The charred faces and cracked skulls of a
Comfortable century. Petal-white sands
Made of tiny shellfish. The crashed motorcycle
Where the sea withdraws with no grief at all.

VI

In dread of the black mountain,
Gratitude for the green mountain.
In dread of the green mountain,
Gratitude for the black mountain.

In dread of the fallen lintel and the ghosted hearth,
        gratitude for the green mountain.
In dread of the crying missile and the jet's chalk,
        gratitude for the black mountain.

In dread of the titled thief, thigh-deep in his name,
        gratitude for the green mountain.
In dread of the neon street to the armed moon,
        gratitude for the black mountain.

In dread of the gilded bible and the rod-cut hand,
        gratitude for the green mountain.
In dread of the uncrossed boards behind the blazing man,
        gratitude for the black mountain.

*

In dread of my shadow on the Green Mountain,
Gratitude for this April of the Black Mountain,
As the grass fountains out of its packed roots,
And a thrush repeats the repertoire of his threats:

> *I hate it, I hate it, I hate it.*
> > *Go away. Go away.*
> *I will not, I will not, I will not.*
> > *Come again. Come again.*

Swifts twist on the syllables of the wind currents.

Blackbirds are the cellos of the deep farms.

# INTERVIEWS

ROLAND MATHIAS was born in 1915 at Talybont-on-Usk, Powys. The family left Wales for Germany and England when Roland was only four, and he did not return to live in Wales until 1948, when he settled in Pembroke Dock. He left again ten years later to teach in Derbyshire and Birmingham, but on his retirement in 1969 came back to live in Brecon. He was co-founder of the *Anglo-Welsh Review*, which he edited 1961-1976. He is the author of six collections of poetry, and his selected poems, *Burning Brambles*, were published in 1983. His other books include a volume of short stories and critical works on Vernon Watkins and John Cowper Powys. He has also edited anthologies of poetry and stories, and a collection of essays on David Jones.

# An Interview with Roland Mathias

—*There is often a sense of exile in your poetry. Presumably this has to do with the fact that you've spent much of your life outside Wales.*

—Yes, I was brought up outside Wales for all but the first four years of my life. When my parents returned to Brecon in 1940 and I was compelled by the intense competition to take a teaching post wherever I could get one (in Lancashire, Reading, Carlisle and London), I could see no likelihood, before 1948, of my returning to Wales, except for holidays.

—*Is the question of exile relevant as well to the relation of your particular generation, and your parents', to Welsh culture, and to the Welsh language?*

—Not to my particular generation, I think; indeed, I have the sensation that I was very much out of step with my contemporaries in wanting to return. Younger generations, including people like John Tripp and Sally Roberts Jones were much more likely to come back. Relevant to my parents, in the obvious sense, of course. I have never been one who rebelled or disparaged or did anything other than remain very attached to them. They were, however, divided in two respects. First, in language and culture. My father was a Carmarthenshire man, Welsh-speaking and very conscious of the validity of Welsh culture. My mother was from east Breconshire, a monoglot English speaker, who inherited that faint disparagement and secret hostility which was characteristic of areas which had lost the Welsh language. I had made sporadic attempts to learn Welsh but never had the time to push them very far. I was conscious that the most I could hope for was my mother's cultural inheritance and even that was denied me by distance. There was a time in the forties when I began research on the matter of recusancy in Herefordshire and Gwent in the seventeeth century, believing that this was my only way back and that geographically these border counties were about as far west as I was likely to get. The second point of division was in relation to the 1939-45 war. My mother was strongly pacifist, my father an Army chaplain who, though no jingoist, accepted the necessity to fight. My brother and I were much influenced by my mother's thinking: we both signed on as conscientious objectors. I was the less fortunate, serving a short prison sentence in 1941 and another of a few days (I was unwillingly bought out by the boys of my then school) in 1942. All this was perhaps the more surprising because in the end I was much more like my father in my interests.

—*How would you describe the meaning of landscape or the sense of place in your poetry?*

—The sense of place in my work is all the stronger because in my childhood I had no permanent home. My father's Army service took us to Germany and to various Army camps like Aldershot and Catterick which were a denial of the civilian community. I never had friends with whom I had grown up and gone to school. At first, then, Wales was the idealised distant community, the more because during my holidays as a student, I spent time with my many cousins — in places like the Rhondda Valley, hard hit by the Depression — and found them lively, generous, and welcoming, despite their circumstances. There was no trace of envy in them for the member of the family who had had all the advantages, including a university education, and now came swanning around to demonstrate them. I put it like that not because I had any such motive, but because I feel the much more envious generation of the present would certainly have seen it like that. It was, in fact, the cheerfulness, the welcome, the sense of community that I found everywhere in Wales that moved me, from the first, to write poems in celebration of these qualities. But I did not know how to do it, not for a very long time. I could come at Wales through landscape or through history, but I did not know how to celebrate its people without sentimentality. And I knew from the beginning that sentimentality had to be avoided. In the event, the relatives whom I would most have liked to know how I felt were, many of them, dead by the time I could find the means to contain the emotion (a case in point is 'They Have Not Survived'). A ridiculous form of incapacity and delay, but there it is. The emotion I felt earlier on pointed itself on Wales and diffused itself on what it could reach.

—*There is often an interesting pattern in your poems to do with the relation of landscape imagery to personal feeling or observation; it involves a kind of expansion, or partial translation, of descriptive meanings into introspective ones. To give some examples, at the end of 'Burning Brambles', the odour of fire becomes 'the smell of a life ill-lived', and the fingers of 'Fool's Fingers' suddenly become those of the poem's speaker, not only the icicles in the landscape of the poem. How in your experience do these different aspects or orders of perception come together, link up?*

—You are getting at my guilt complex, I think. In terms of poetry, this is partly connected with what I've just said, but it is much more a product of my Puritan upbringing. All my life I have made complacency my enemy. Pomposity and self-satisfaction are real sins to me. I have *not* done what I should, not lived my life according to the precepts which I know to be right. In old-fashioned terminology, I am as convicted of sin as most of my forbears. But I do not regard this as a handicap as a writer. It is rather the first step towards doing better. Or certainly towards doing, that is, trying again. There is in me a constant urge towards the Christian ideal which is not in the least pious (note the few poems I have written that can possibly be called devotional). I 'distinguish' myself most of all by knowing that I have had advantages not given to many and have made little of them. It is, I think, not unnatural that I should look at Nature and then turn, with a grimace, aware of myself as the spectre at the feast,

—*Your poetic language is surely the most acrobatic — full of leaps, twists, sudden rhythmic and semantic couplings ('tripright', 'bloodwreck') — of any poet writing in English in Wales. Does this partly reflect your interest in Hopkins? In general, what poets or poetic traditions do you feel the closest affinities with?*

—Hopkins, yes. The first poet to excite me rather than move me to tears. The amazing rhythms, the tautness. But this was very early on. I knew I had to get away from Hopkins, as from every other poet. I think perhaps my early study of Browning ought to be mentioned. He, too, was acrobatic, if also rougher than Hopkins. And I, too, have been accused of being deliberately rough and unmusical. I've never thought about this till recently, but I think maybe there's a clue there. Other poets like Tennyson and A.E. Housman moved me, too — I was always aware of the power of Tennyson's cadence — but I was always afraid of going too hard after them because of the danger of sentimentality. I am, in fact, very sentimental, but have always known that to let this into my poetry would be to slacken its tautness and weaken its power. In that sense, then, I've always been a poet with the brake on.

—*Often the juxtapositions in your language create an ironic effect through a contrast of tone. For example, in the phrase 'my heart fidgets off' from 'Burning Brambles', 'heart' with something blander, more predictable might seem sentimental, and likewise in the case of 'fidgets', which might sound too whimsical. And at the end of 'Freshwater West Revisited', the blunt, even prosaic quality of the phrase 'lays the action bare' tends to make the shock of 'bloodwreck' more dramatic. Would you comment on this?*

—Again, it has partly to do with resistance to sentimentality. The combination of *heart* and *fidgets* — yes, ironic. But the two words are not separate effects shoved together. I thought of my heart as fidgeting — that is, its typical movement was frivolous and unconcentrated. I wrote 'lays the action bare' as a *hard* phrase and its intention, indeed, was to toughen up *'bloodwreck'*, which I regard as a bit dubious and overblown (even filmic, perhaps). The main thing here and in many other poems was to avoid the merely pretty and to convey, as powerfully as may be, emotions and actions which might not be pretty at all but were truer.

—*A recurring concern in your poems is that of survival, its difficulty, its conditions.*

—Survival. I really don't think this figures much in my work except that the failure of the worthy to survive is a matter for profound regret. I'm interested in *tradition*, what makes it and how, if worthy, it can be made to persist. I take the view, for example, that myth is a changed or perverted version of history — not some power in its own right. Here again I am puritanical, political, and realistic. To me Christianity has to meet the world in the terms that men will understand, not mysteriously from behind a cloud of incense. But, broadly, to come back to the point, I see so many good things dying in the name of progress and unworthy motives raised to the name of intelligence.

—*How has your involvement with history affected your poetry and your relation with Wales?*

—Like many of your questions, I find this a difficult one to answer. What I can remember is this. When I began teaching (in England) I also started some research into recusancy in Herefordshire and Monmouthshire, basically because I came across a volume of the Salisbury papers which contained much information on that subject. I believed (rather pitifully, perhaps, in view of my later return to Wales) that I was, in professional terms, shut out from my native country and I therefore grabbed at any aspect of Welsh history which seemed congenial because in and through it I *could* return, could participate intellectually, at least, in the continuum of Wales. I was oppressed by the fact that I was without the Welsh my father had and, in my gloomier moments, persuaded myself that the border area I was working on was probably all I deserved, all I could culturally hope for. As I think about what I've just said, it seems emotionally overstated and unlikely, but I believe it to be broadly true to the nagging feeling of deprivation from which I then suffered.

When I returned to Wales it was to Pembrokeshire and English-speaking

Pembrokeshire at that. Nevertheless, I was *back* and the literary activity in which I was soon engaged (with *Dock Leaves*) did much to remove the earlier pain. The feeling that circumstances had made me an outsider persisted, however, and a poem like 'Porth Cwyfan' reveals that, for all my knowledge of the history of Wales, I felt that it was not enough to make me the Welshman I very much wanted to be. I was perhaps ('How is my tripright sounder?') only one degree removed from the casual tourist.

— *What do you think about the poet and his role?*

—I am less certain about this, in the Anglo-Welsh context, than I was, say, ten years ago. The moment, in some indefinable way, has passed. What I think no longer has that stamp of practicality about it that it once appeared to have. Nevertheless, I say what I have to say, because it belongs to me and I can say no other.

I have very little use for confessional poetry, written in the tiresome belief that the poet's experiences are in some way unique. I join with David Jones in thinking that what the poet has is not unique experience and sensibility but the craftsman's ability to turn that experience into poetry and the mental ability and sympathy to make that experience as much universal as personal. The poet, as I see him, is a man in place and time, subject to both as all people are, but capable of interpreting that place and time and himself in both, in the light of the pattern of history and social change, conscious always of what has been most of all because he remembers what he once was and why. In the Anglo-Welsh context this means, for me, remembering the Wales that was, recalling its roots in the Welsh language and in the values of the society that that language informed — not in some hopelessly nostalgic fashion nor in the manner of one who is out to condemn the present, but in the belief that *knowing* what is past and feeling it still within the bones will defend the real values of that past and make it plainer what course or courses the present should pursue with honour. Those hostile to this concept would call it a natural conservatism (though always, I hope, with a small *c*): those more favourable might be willing to have it described as a sense of history in the immediate, which evaluates both foolish trends and progressive opportunities in the light of what an honourable and caring society can suffer to happen. Literarily, Anglo-Welsh poetry cannot survive under that name, in my view, unless it is in some sense concerned with the existence of a Welsh identity. It is unlikely to go back now to the Welsh language for its momentum, but a total lack of interest in Welsh history, tradition and literature (in translation, if the work be in Welsh) must necessarily indicate, in due course, a fall-back to models exclusively English or transatlantic. The poetry may not be worse poetry because that happens, but it can no longer be Anglo-Welsh.

All this indicates, I suppose, that I am a political and social animal, not an ivory-tower romantic. So be it. I cannot take a poetic position in which the trials of the ego are of more importance and interest than the fate of the national and cultural group to which I belong.

ROBERT MINHINNICK was born in Neath in 1952, but spent his childhood in the village of Pen-y-fai, near Bridgend. He has mixed formal education, including the research for a thesis on David Jones, with a variety of jobs, including one with a salvage company in Cardiff's dockland. He now lives on the Glamorgan coast at Porthcawl. Robert Minhinnick has published three collections of poetry, the latest being *Life Sentences* (1983).

# An Essay by Robert Minhinnick

I write a poem seeking to understand something, hoping to make something, and wishing to communicate that. For instance, I have written several poems about a man I knew who committed suicide. I don't think I ever discovered, writing the poems, 'why' he killed himself, or ever glimpsed the 'truth' of that event — what really happened. But I developed and presented a 'version' of the truth. I needed to write about that man. It was an emotional and intellectual need. It came out of horror and fascination and love. I can't explain that very well because all the words are already in the poems. Writing those poems was something I knew I would do, I was convinced of it.

At that same period I used to work with my grandfather at a job salvaging waste-paper. We worked in a derelict garage in the village where we lived, and a potent memory is of the cold working its way into the core of my body. There were usually fifteen-foot stacks of green and white computer print-outs around us, and we would pull out the carbon from between the doubled sheets. There must have been miles of carbon paper that we had to burn in an incinerator in a field behind the garage. Our hands and faces and clothes grew black from the carbon. We looked like miners, working in this garage — Smith's garage — surrounded by paper, rusting engines, tanks of oil and lubricating grease. While we worked my grandfather told me stories about the village. He told me about adventures of his boyhood, mining, playing rugby, working as a gardener, about strikes and poverty and hunger, and the way things like houses, streets, farms, and then people, used to look before time changed them. I was always interested in what he said, but some things would strike home, lodge in my mind, one story or description in twenty years perhaps, and I knew, I was sure, I would write about them. And they became my experiences, part of my life. One story was about catching trout in a stream in 1921, the year of a great miners' strike. The way he described it, quickly but carefully, artfully in the best sense, allowed me to see, quite vividly, *his* hands in the brookwater, the fish he had caught lying on the grassy stream-bank, his effort and his triumph. And of course I saw *my* hands in the current, and the fish *I* had caught stranded on the bank dying in the moonlight — my own triumph. As in the life of the man who committed suicide, I could see my own life.

I suppose I recognised what we shared, understood our inescapable fellowship. But I know I wrote the poem about the trout quite quickly after hearing the story. Probably I had the carbon stains on my hands when I wrote it, because it was always difficult to scrub them off. My grandfather read the poem when it was printed and said he was pleased with it, but of course it could never truly recreate that event in his life. Instead, it created a new one in my own, and possibly in his. Perhaps it could be said that I merely use such stories as raw material for poetry, but that would be only partly true. The poem could never serve as a simple mirror-image of my grandfather catching trout. Recently I did a poetry reading at the University of Georgetown in Washington. When I arrived there I was surprised that some of the students had been studying this poem, and after the reading one of the students said how much he liked the way I compared the weather in the poem — a very long hot dry spell in which it was easy to catch trout — to the 'political climate', the fact that a very bitter industrial strike was in progress. The student claimed that the poem was obviously political, and this surprised me. I'd never looked at the poem in that way — perhaps a confession of naivety — but I was pleased that someone who had read the poem had experienced it on levels I wasn't conscious of when writing it. If I had been asked to explain the poem, I would have done so in a way different from the student's. That is why I think it best not to enquire too deeply of myself why I write poetry. After all, when the poem is read it becomes part of the reader's sense of reality, which will never totally correspond with that of the writer. In describing the trout and the hot weather I perhaps gave them more 'importance' than they possessed. A poem can be destroyed by the writer looking for significances and depending on them, rather than fresh and original language. But this poem, stemming from second-hand experience shows, I hope, that where the poem comes from is not particularly important. My reaction will be to treat different subjects the same way. And one description of that process is my effort to concentrate on the dramatic quality, the dynamic in an experience, and present it in a way in which the reader will feel himself involved, or inevitably drawn into. I might say I wish to make the reader part of the poem, but perhaps that's going too far.

I feel Welsh but I wasn't brought up to speak the language. The Welsh I know I've learned slowly and painfully. I've lived in this country all my life and think it a good place to be a poet and to write poetry, but to be obsessed with my national identity would be boring and unhealthy. Wales is a country of strongly creative frictions, at least I feel they should be creative, especially for writers. The rural and the industrial, traditional industry and new technology, the English and the Welsh languages, a past representing an emphatic and unique cultural identity and a present in which that identity might become irreversibly eroded. I enjoy the work of many Welshmen who write in English, and feel a great sympathy, a sense of 'commonality' with Alun Lewis, Dylan Thomas and Roland Mathias for example. Those three are very different types of writers but I see many things that link their work. What is first noticeable is their precision, the scrupulous use of words, and the fact that their obvious deliberation does not constrict them, nor dim their fire. These are three of the Welsh writers I enjoy, but if I had to mention influences, they would span very many forms of writing, most recently, perhaps, *Lyrical Ballads* , especially Wordsworth's social probing, and his portrayal of memorable individual figures; the ordinary rendered unique. Certainly I feel myself part of an English language tradition in Wales which these three represent, a tradition established only in this century. Most of my poems are about Wales, or more specifically, the people I know in Wales. I use them as subjects because they are what surrounds me.

Probably the student in Washington was right when he said I write political poetry (sometimes), but in a very oblique fashion. My neighbours are real people with individual identities before they are instruments used to depict what Welsh life is like in the twentieth century. 'Smith's Garage' might be said to be political, in the sense that you could see the description of a derelict industrial site as a metaphor for the present state of Wales. But that would be too easy. What interested me in writing the poem, what excited and impelled me to write was the extraordinary interaction between the natural world and the industrial in that garage. There were gear-wheels and fly-wheels scattered around the yard, all orange with rust. And they looked exactly like the enormous gilled fungi that sprouted there in the grass. Where the dynamos had worked all day in the garage there was a thrush singing. Before it was taken away for scrap, a yellow bulldozer was parked in a corner. It had completely seized up and was covered in brambles and nettles. But there was nothing incongruous in that sight. As I say in the poem, the industrial had 'fused' into the natural. There was now no clear division between them. The oil on the floor looked like the glassy-green encroachment of ivy leaves. I had seen such things at Smith's Garage every day for years. But one day I called there and *noticed* them for the first time. And I knew I would write about them. It was a tremendous feeling, a release, a discovery. I felt marvellous but not because I could draw a parallel between Wales and the abandoned garage workshop. It was the rusted gear-wheels that delighted me, the exhaust systems trailing bindweed and couch-grass, the chalk marks of ancient lorry rotas viewed through a nest of webs. There was a harmony there, a sense of destiny fulfilled. And the physical reality seemed far more important than the theoretical possibilities of the scene.

JOHN TRIPP was born in the Rhymney Valley at Bargoed in 1927 and now lives in Whitchurch, a suburb of Cardiff. His varied career as a journalist, copy-writer and embassy information officer took him to London until 1968 when he returned to Wales as a free-lance journalist. One of his jobs was literary editor of *Planet*. He has published six volumes of poetry since his first, *Diesel to Yesterday* in 1966. John Tripp appeared in the Penguin Modern Poets series in 1979, a year after his *Collected Poems* had been published. A new collection, *Passing Through*, appeared in 1984.

# An Interview with John Tripp

*—You are generally considered the only truly urban poet writing in Wales today. How did your urban orientation come about, and how important do you feel a consideration of the urban aspects of Wales is to an overall view of the country?*

—I've always lived and worked in the urban areas, and my experience stems from this time spent in mining valleys, London and Cardiff. The urban aspects of Wales are important to an overall view because when we say 'urban' here we mean, usually, South Wales, where most of the population live, where much of the old wealth was made — mostly by outsiders in iron, coal and shipping — and where poverty has been dire. As a boy in the Rhymney Valley, and later in Cardiff, I witnessed much distress and hardship. I have not forgotten it.

*—How do you view the relationship between the urban and rural in Wales: do the two aspects have anything positive to offer each other, or are they by nature antipathetic?*

—The urban and rural should have something positive to say to each other, as we are one country, if not a united 'nation' due to the language barrier and the anglicized influence. But rural themes were always thought to be more 'poetic' than urban ones, set among the aerials and housing estates. The pastoral has had a fatal attraction for many Welsh poets, to the exclusion of all else — just as the cliches of pit and chapel have maimed other poets. I prefer a landscape with figures, on the whole.

*—Has your experience of Wales affected your urban perspective or vision? You concentrate, for instance, mainly on small town urbanism rather than the metropolis.*

—My experience of Wales affected my urban perspective in that my particular brand of patriotism could see the rot setting in down south, and elsewhere, and I observed and meditated on this dereliction and sadness through empathy with the people in towns and wrecked mining villages where hope seems to have vanished. Seeing and feeling this, I could hardly by-pass the modern urban experience in an industrial wasteland by simply contemplating rabbits, the ways of foxes and other rural delights. But perhaps the theme chose me, not the reverse. No pre-selected vision, so to speak, was involved.

Of course, the Welsh sources of my urbanism were reinforced by the twenty years I spent in London as a journalist and researcher. I walked down some mean streets, met a lot of interesting and unfortunate people, and sometimes didn't see anything green for weeks, except in the parks. One of the most rewarding things was meeting other writers I respected and admired — Amis, Alvarez, Wesker, the poets Fleur Adcock and Patricia Beer, and others. I also enjoyed the company of foreign correspondents in Fleet Street bars and fellow sub-editors at the BBC, who taught me something about concision and economy. These were exciting urban days.

Probably this metropolitan experience, coupled with whatever imagination and perception I possessed, helped me to handle urban subject matter and prepared me for coping with the social, political and cultural shambles of Wales when I returned. That was about fifteen years ago, and since then the main content of my work has been that traditional Anglo-Welsh imagery of pit, chapel and cinema, recast in present-day terms: the now-dead pit, the empty chapel, the cinema-turned-bingo hall. These images are often counterpointed with very different impressions: the images of glossy, expensive hotels, sumptuous food, the pointless pomp and ritual of royal visits. And a rural element also figures at times, in the recollection of visits to old monasteries deep in the countryside, I love the isolation and peace of those places. My other rural excursions have mostly involved glimpses of lost ways of life — seeing abandoned farms or watching an obsolete plough-man. I'm no bucolic romantic, I try to look at the countryside from the worker's, the grafter's viewpoint. Best to leave the romance to lovers of the pastoral.

*—But how did you get this particular mixture of material to work as poetry?*

—In that regard, I probably owe a good deal to the influence of T.S. Eliot. I was very much under his influence during my London days and, to some extent, I still am. I used to read his essays as if they were revelation, and I have never forgotten his famous description of how poetic imagination works — 'When a poet's mind is perfectly equipped for its work, it is constantly amalgamating disparate experience; the ordinary man's experience is chaotic, irregular, fragmentary. The latter falls in love, or reads Spinoza, and these two experiences have nothing to do with each other, or with the noise of the type-writer, or the smell of cooking; in the mind of the poet these experiences are always forming new wholes.' This notion of juxtaposing disparate elements seemed right in approaching the historical mess in Wales, it was the 'objective correlative' I was looking for.

*—Were there any other models or affinities that gave support or justification for the track you wanted to take, Charles Olson or William Carlos Williams, for example? Also W.H. Davies perhaps, given his urban themes?*

—Yes, I did find support in all those people, especially the Americans. I'd read old W.H. Davies, of course, and both Olson and Williams had worked in ways that reinforced the direction I intended to follow. There were several oblique influences — R.S. Thomas, obviously, but even Lowell's confessional honesty had its place here, as well as the West Indian Derek Walcott and his marvellous awareness of roots, colonial history and his compassion even for the ruling exploiters.

*—Did your strong nationalist feeling have any very specific relationship to your development as a poet?*

—Most of my work has had a patriotic-nationalist centre which made my loyalties pretty clear. Certainly this provided one of the motivating energies in my work, but there's always the danger when dealing with political or social themes that you can easily lose control. The end-product can come across as bluster, posturing or discursiveness. I've continually worked to correct this, with some invaluable help from critics like Jeremy Hooker, Roland Mathias and John Pikoulis, who helped sharpen my awareness of the importance of tone.

*—Besides a strong patriotism are there any other particularly Welsh aspects to your work?*

—Besides the patriotism, which is still there but not as strong as it was before the disastrous Referendum on Devolution in '79, other Welsh aspects of my work are an authentic sense of place and a genuine concern for the underdog, the marginal people in our botched society, the neglected and forgotten. At our best, we *do* care...

*—Your sense of place often has an occasional quality to it which nevertheless can be quite evocative*

*and intense in feeling. By this I mean that the experience of place for you is often the occasion of an encounter with the past, as in 'Epitaph at Gilfach Goch', 'At Bosherston Ponds' and 'Penarth' — all poems which combine personal reflection or reminiscence with a sense of the history of the place. Perhaps something similar happens in other kinds of encounters as well, in poems like 'Scratch Farmer', 'Ploughman' and 'Soil', but there is less of a personal and subjective note in these.*

—It's true that some of my 'place' poems often stem from a brief encounter with the past. I wrote 'Epitaph at Gilfach Goch' and an earlier poem, 'Where the Rainbow Ends', after visiting Gilfach Goch with a friend who was born and brought up there. I was very moved by what I saw and heard: this once-thriving mining community that dug so much coal for the world, now quiet and 'greened over' as part of the new landscaping experiment. I saw old ghosts, the village as it once had been, which inspired Richard Llewellyn's *How Green Was My Valley*. It inspired me, too — the busy, hard past compared with the empty present, a history of a race, and my own relation to the place because I'd been born in a town very much like it, Bargoed in the Rhymney Valley. It was all there — the hopes, the toil, the grief and sadness. A similar kind of remembrance of things past is involved in 'At Bosherston Ponds' and 'Penarth', the former set in coastal Pembrokeshire among those ancient lily-ponds, and the latter in our local seaside bolt-hole with its pebbly beach, an escape route to a few hours of sunny or rainy enjoyment. It is when the historical and the personal truly engage that I start to fire on all cylinders, as it were. 'Scratch Farmer', 'Ploughman' and 'Soil' are less subjective poems: I tried with these to convey a modest sense of loss for what has gone, the old rural skills, though one shouldn't regret too much the passing of a very hard and sometimes calamitous way of life.

One of the oddities to do with poems about places is the way that certain out-of-the-way spots can trigger off a poem while others, often lovelier, or famous as landmarks, can leave one cold. There are corners of my own village, Eglwys Newydd (as in the poem of that name), which still draw me back after all these years — the derelict workshops, cinema, back lanes, littered brook, over-grown Victorian graveyard — which were there before the flash supermarket and the junk food joints. Also many other places, little lost territories in Wales and England. It's almost as if we continue to see people there before their habitats collapsed and another generation took over.

*—Is your tendency to frame the past in the present, or vice versa — at any rate your insistence on their mutual presence — is this also a reflection of your affinity with Eliot's observations? Or, to put it another way, does the idea of combining heterogeneous elements have a strongly historical slant for you?*

—Yes, I agree this could derive from my affinity with Eliot's observations — a touch of 'East Coker' perhaps, or 'Chard Witlow' as Henry Reed parodied it! But Eliot, and Auden to a certain extent, taught how it was possible to try to bring some sanity to the present by understanding the past, and how one damned thing led to another. Without a sense of history, it's like walking without your shadow. And especially in Wales: there's always brooding history at the back of what's happening, trying to squeeze into the centre of a modern frame.

*—Is the idea of combining a variety of elements in your work a reflection for you of a necessary*

*condition of modernism, or of the nature of urban experience or a condition of personal truth?*

—Probably it represents all of those things, they naturally interlock. Our contemporary world is hopelessly fragmented ('these fragments I have shored against my ruin'), so maybe my poetry is an attempt at some sort of order in chaos, an effort to 'sellotape' together a baffling multiplicity of fragments. Impossible, of course, but it may pass the time.

*— Your style involves several elements that most readers familiar with your work would recognize: irony, humour, directness of language, immediate sense impressions and observations. Did this style come naturally to you, or have you worked at it in certain ways? Do you aim for a certain tone? Do you write your poems pretty much at one go — in a hotel room, or in a restaurant, as the poems themselves often seem to suggest?*

—On the whole my style came naturally to me, but I've worked on it through the years — aiming for a certain tone that's more 'slow left-arm spin' that 'fast bumpers' that knock the reader out. My poems often begin on the backs of envelopes or in a little notebook in hotels, bars (when still sober!), restaurants, trains — hardly ever at home in a quiet room. I've started drafts of poems in a stationary car in Llantwit Major, in Selfridges' cafe, in Berni's cafe in Caerffili, all over. The real slog comes later, the revising, polishing, then another close look when typing. I try to achieve a style of sparseness and concision in dealing with my themes — or rather, as I've said, the themes that have chosen me. I wanted, ideally, in my poems to create a terse, epigrammatic commentary on the Wales of today, its ramshackle beauty and sadness, its cultural and political predicament, its pride. If my work embodies any kind of philosophy, it is one that, though personal and deeply felt, has very much to do with what I have been able to perceive and express about a very particular nation and world.

GILLIAN CLARKE was born in 1937 in Cardiff. In recent years she has divided her time between her home there and Cardiganshire, where, during 1984-85 she is Writer in Residence at St. David's University College, Lampeter. Between 1976 and 1984 she edited the *Anglo-Welsh Review*. Her three collections of poems are *Snow on the Mountain* (1971), *The Sundial* (1978) and *Letter from a Far Country* (1982).

# An Interview with Gillian Clarke

*—To begin with 'Letter from a Far Country', what were some of the motivating forces behind the poem, other than the fact that it was a commission from the Welsh Arts Council and the BBC?*
—Before I had the commission, I had been considering the idea of writing a novel about women, about three generations of women. I had in mind first my grandmother, her rural life, her thorough Welshness, and the pressure on her to conform absolutely to the respectability of those days. Then my mother, swamped in a sense of inferiority about being Welsh and trying with all her might to be English. And the next generation rediscovering Welshness and pride in it, which is somehow parallel to the new confidence of women and of the women's movement. Then along came the commission and the idea shaped itself as a half-hour poem. In fact, whenever I try to write anything, it ends up as a poem.

*—You have previously mentioned anger as a catalyst in this poem.*
—Really the anger arose because of the difficulty of actually writing the poem. I realized when I did it that I couldn't do anything at a long stretch because I had so many duties, so many things that broke up my day, because of working in a house. Nobody regards a house as a place where work is going on. The place of work which was my study, my cooking room, my thinking room was a place of enormous interruption. The anger eventually was against those who assumed I had all the time in the world and that all women have all the time in the world to do things simply because they live in a house and work in a house which is clearly a place where nothing goes on. It was also to do with the low valuation that is given to what women do.

People sometimes ask 'Well, what do you do?' and I tell them, and they say, 'Now why don't women write great works? Why aren't they great painters?' It's a very annoying question, because women *have* produced 'Great Art'. There is Emily Dickinson and Jane Austen and George Eliot — and the long list of women painters who were until very recently actually left out of the history of art. So 'where are your great works?' became a central idea. But it's very difficult to argue about such things without getting angry. I thought the best thing to do was to make it amusing. So I hope its place in the poem does that. People laugh when I read it; sometimes it's better to quote foolish questions instead of answering them.

*—You yourself have described 'Letter from a Far Country' as an epic poem about housework. Some people would question whether such a poem is possible.*
—An epic poem about housework — why not? If the work of raising the generations is not epic, what is? If trenches, guns, blood are fit for poetry, as in the work of David Jones, why not kitchens, jam, nappies, birth! It's a question of the size of the creative ideas you ask these bits and pieces to carry. I reckoned I had enough emotional force and a large enough creative idea for using such paraphernalia and making poetry of it. All creative energy is the same. If you bake brown bread and gather bluebells, and paint a picture with a child, the head of steam is taken off that energy, the poem will wait until tomorrow. Think of the last century, the letters women wrote, the journals, the samplers, the embroidery, the bread, the preserves, the quality of

efficiency and passion they put into a day's work. There was neither patronage nor audience nor record, but it was civilized and creative and a close relation to art. So I hope I've taken that work and put it into a poem that is art. Yet a critic wrote 'in spite of its domestic subject...' in praising 'Letter'. Why should the domestic not be a suitable subject for art? Did they say that to Van Gogh, 'in spite of that domestic subject... that chair, those flowers..'? So the fact that some people said it was a 'good poem, but' meant they were actually making lists of what you are and are not allowed to write about — which is a complete justification for the feminist argument that there is nothing to stop women being as great writers as men except the shortlist of acceptable topics.

—*Has your knowledge of Welsh influenced your poetry, or is your work more influenced by English literature?*

—That's an enormous and complicated question. My loss of Welsh has been a very strong tension in my writing. But English is my mother tongue, and it is the tongue I was educated in. But being a woman and Welsh and therefore in two senses not wholly ready to count myself as one of the grown-ups, not easily able to feel I was permitted to be myself, to be a writer, an artist, I was a very late developer. Many women, particularly in Wales, are late developers as writers. I didn't begin writing properly until I was thirty, by which time I had long been learning Welsh. So, while I grew through childhood and adolescence without Welsh, I already knew a lot of Welsh before I began to write openly. I began to write and to post poems because of the existence of the Welsh magazines written in English, like the *Anglo-Welsh Review*, *Poetry Wales*, and others. Those magazines gave me a sense of my own ability to join the ranks of the writers within them, writers who seemed to be giving me, written down, my own world.

So in one sense, the woman writer begins to write coming across Sylvia Plath, Anne Sexton, Anne Stevenson; in another sense, the writer begins to write coming across poetry written by other Welsh people in the English language. And these two sources converging gave me more of a sense that I could write as well. As I began to read Welsh poetry in translation, and then in the original language with the help of translations, and as I heard conversations mainly in Cardiganshire between Welsh people around me, between the farmers in the landscape which I regard very much as my landscape now — how else, what else would one be but influenced? The stories I heard the farmers tell were in Welsh, and they come into my poems in English. Also, I'm very fond of the seven syllable line, and I've got that from Dafydd ap Gwilym, and from others like him, though not necessarily consciously. And I don't use rhymes at the endings of lines, but at other places in the line, and that, too, is a very Welsh characteristic. I love using *cynghanedd*; I don't do this regularly as the Welsh-language poets do, but I let it happen and feel a private pleasure in it. It is something that puts an extra tremor or richness into the line. Also, occasionally the word that comes into a poem is a Welsh one, as in one poem where I use the word 'dŵr' instead of water, because it was the right one to use on that occasion.

—*Would you say something about the current direction of your work?*

—When I wrote 'Letter from a Far Country', I wrote it very, very intensively, in five nights, beginning at midnight and writing through until about two in the morning, so I wrote it very quickly and at the last minute. When you write like that, you release something that's actually pretty deeply within your memory and imagination. And by writing something long instead of the usual short, shaped, forged thing that I had been writing, I realized that digging deep was an important way forward for me. Going into the past, going deeper, going down through the layers became important. I was mining my own memory, my family's memory and Welsh memory as far as I could, within the restrictions of a half-hour poem. That's more important to me. That is how I am writing now, because the past informs what we are now.

*—How are you going about this? Are you following up certain themes or ideas?*

—I decided to research the history of my own family to discover how it reflected what has happened to social patterns in Wales and the history of Wales. I am in fact a fairly good model for what's happened, since my own family history is a typical one. By beavering about in old graveyards and in parish registers and in archives, I have found the sort of richness that you can find if you look into myth, the extra meanings, stories and symbolism used by many writers. My favourite writers such as David Jones and Yeats have done it in their several ways. I found there was enough of that kind of thing in Wales' history, in the history of just one tribe, to give me books and books of poems.

The other thing I am certain of since writing 'Letter from a Far Country' is that the right way forward is to be more and not less oneself. If I'm Welsh, and if I'm a woman, then what I must not try to be is a perfect English man poet and to model myself on what's going on among the men.

*—Have there been any immediate or specific influences on what you're writing now?*

—One major and direct influence has been the *Cofiant*.

*—Could you describe what that is?*

—In the last century there arose a very strange kind of book. Someone would gather together the letters, sermons, and a family history concerning the person who was the subject of the *Cofiant*. These would be collected together in a book, called a *Cofiant*, which means remembrances. The subject was often a clergyman, the writer a friend or relative. The one in my family was written by a man who bears my own father's name, John Penri Williams. It was published in 1895, and was written about his father, my great, great grandfather, the Reverend Thomas Williams who was born in 1800 in the Llyn peninsula in North Wales. The *Cofiant* shows that they had not moved from that rural community and were still living in the same family farm as they had been for many, many generations. Further research told me that the family living in this farm had descended from the minor gentry — and although it's well known that in Tudor times gentlemen made up genealogies to fill up the empty hours, nevertheless, if we are to believe the particular Tudor gentleman in my family, then this little tribe of farmers was descended from the Welsh princes. Whether they were or whether they weren't is irrelevant, because it contains in any case, a marvellous image of what has happened to Wales. The genealogy is a thing of great beauty, there are marvellous names: Gwynedd, Madoc, Angharad and Princess Nest. Suddenly in 1725 an English surname is imposed.

I thought it would be possible to go to the very places mentioned in the *Cofiant* , to walk down the road and see the line of the hill that Thomas Williams saw as he walked there when he was six years old and was being taken from his mother to go and live with an aunt; to cross a field and recognize a hawthorn tree, a little bridge where this stream meets that stream and know it must be the place where he was baptized when he was twenty.

*—So you've been able to find most of the places?*

—Yes, because Wales is old and hasn't changed and the crossroads are still where the crossroads were, and the farms still have their names and the mountains have their names. I found all the places, I have not failed to find any of them.

*—One last question, could you describe how poems usually begin for you?*

—I do not need to be hurt into poetry, as Yeats put it. Neither do I need ideas, as such. I store things in memory. The red and white hens and other images from 'Letter', for example, have been in my memory since early childhood. I have kept journals and diaries since I was fifteen, and I re-read them and things spring to life and poetry from those pages. I take photographs and make what I call my picture books. Looking at them reminds me there are things I want to write about when the image/energy/idea meet at the right force.

Then there's the sheet of paper. There are *words*, the paraphernalia of words, books, sermons, conversations, eavesdroppings, notebooks, pens. After pen and paper, the beauty of the empty cleanness, there is energy. It sets me thinking. I try the paper to see what the words will do. It must be like drawing... try the line, see what happens.

JEREMY HOOKER is one of the 'outsiders' in the book, being born near Southampton in 1941. He moved to Wales in 1965 as a lecturer in English at University College, Aberystwyth, where he made an influential contribution to Anglo-Welsh literature. His critical works include volumes on John Cowper Powys and David Jones and a collection of essays on various writers. The latest of his five volumes of poetry, *Englishman's Road* (1980), is largely concerned with the influence of Wales on him as a poet. Jeremy Hooker moved to Holland in 1984.

# An Interview with Jeremy Hooker

—*Your poetry has a highly visual quality; is there any particular background to this?*

—I think it must arise in the first instance from the fact that my father was (and is) a fine landscape painter, so that from the beginning I've been surrounded by paintings, they've been a natural part of my life. Also, the work of a number of other painters means a great deal to me, both those in the English tradition — Paul Nash among modern painters, and Samuel Palmer, Constable and the Norwich School earlier on — and the work of especially the more realistic European painters, as diverse as Jan Van Eyck and Millet. On the other hand, a lot of the writing I responded to most acutely has strong visual elements. One of the strongest literary influences upon me from an early age was Richard Jefferies, who's highly visual in his images, as indeed, is the Imagist Movement in poetry. And for that matter, a great deal of English poetry has strong visual qualities. In addition, there's the very strong emphasis I place upon the matter of seeing: first of all, seeing physically that which is all around us and immediately in front of us, and attempting to express that as vividly and as accurately as possible with regard to the nature of what is being seen. But also there is the moral value of seeing which is very much a part of the Romantic movement in its broadest sense. And within the Romantic movement, there's a strong realist element that emphasizes seeing things accurately and sharply and valueing their otherness. So within that tradition, too, great value is placed upon the visual, upon the quality of seeing. In his book on Richard Jefferies, Edward Thomas speaks eloquently about the moral value of seeing, and of the relationship between seeing and imagination. He makes the point that seeing clearly is a function of the imagination, and a function of a love of the world in the things that we're seeing. And I believe that to see things as clearly and as vividly as we can is an expression of the degree to which we value them carefully.

—*Other sense impressions, not only the visual, are important in your work. What part in the creative process do these play for you?*

—They are often important in the genesis of a poem. Many of my poems begin from experience outdoors. I've very seldom written poems that are contained so to speak between the floor and the ceiling — most of my poems take place between the earth and the sky. Many of them have their seeds in walks in the countryside, they don't necessarily immediately follow upon the experience, but the sense impression may remain dormant and then be recalled at a later period. I think sense impressions must play an important part in the work of any poet who values an acute sense of the physical world, it's necessarily so, and I think that if my poems were entirely visual they would have a flatness, a one-dimensionality. Many of my poems arise from what I call pre-literary experience, from the very physical experience of walking along a shingle beach, or dipping my hand in water, or feeling rain falling upon me and running down my neck, or handling a piece of wood of a particular shape. It doesn't mean the poem is necessarily about any of those things, but that those things have some effect upon my imagination that makes me want to find a verbal correspondence to the physical experience, and then the images which arise in relation to this experience will often attract to them other images from the past, or from the experience of other people that I've heard or read about. As far as I'm concerned, a large part of the creative process is pretty mysterious, and I don't much want to look into it. All I know is I have a strong feeling for the physical world which is a sense of touch as well as a sense of sight and smell and hearing, and that this feeling has a very close relationship to the fact that I write poetry and to the kind of poetry I write. But there are certain mysteries in the transaction between sense impression and word that I've got no wish to look into very closely.

*— You don't yourself understand this entirely then?*

—I wouldn't want to understand the process too clearly; I think if one did there wouldn't be any compulsion to write. I don't want to indulge in unnecessary mystification about it, but I think it's the experience of most poets, however conscious they may be of their art, however much they may be theorists, that there is an area of darkness that surrounds the creative process.

*— You've written quite a lot on English-language writers of Wales. To what extent have such writers had a bearing on your own work?*

—They've had quite a strong bearing. This is a difficult question, because the importance to me of the Anglo-Welsh writers is very great, and it's not single or simple either, I would say in the first place I feel quite an affinity with some Anglo-Welsh writers, notably David Jones and R.S. Thomas, but also Alun Lewis, and a number of the younger Anglo-Welsh poets. This arises in part from some sense that my relationship with my own primary place, with England, has something in common with their ambiguous position of belonging and at the same time not belonging, existing in a kind of territory between belonging and not belonging that characterizes their relationship with Wales. Of course, I admire a great deal of Anglo-Welsh poetry as poetry, and this was so before I came to Wales and knew anything at all about the special conditions that prevail here.

It is significant for me that the emphases of Anglo-Welsh writing are in the main different from the emphases of a lot of writing, perhaps the majority of writing, by my contemporaries, and for that matter, the previous generation of poets in England. I feel closer to the position of the Anglo-Welsh poets in relation to their subjects, and their attitude and outlook than I do to most, though not all, of my English contemporaries.

*— This idea of the poet having a basically affirmative relation to society is important, because one often thinks of the poet or artist as an alienated rebel, so that it's become a kind of cliché, an idée fixe to the extent that it's assumed this attitude is an inalienable pre-condition to the creative process.*

—I think that idea of the poet *has* become a cliché. Yet one should say straightaway there are very good historical reasons for estrangement and alienation, and a powerful literature in Europe and America in the twentieth century which has arisen out of that situation. Nowadays, wherever we might live, it's very difficult for any of us to entirely escape being alienated and estranged, both from other people and from something in ourselves. This is a complicated matter because even poets such as myself, who are reacting strongly against alienation and estrangement nevertheless share to some extent in the condition to which they're reacting. Indeed, because they share in it, and don't like it, that's one reason they're reacting against it.

There is in Wales certainly an alternative tradition which I've found most refreshing. In Wales, the isolation that's inevitably attendant upon any artist is balanced by the feeling for community that the poet has. There is here the idea that the poet is a man in society — for me as an English poet, I relate this to the Wordsworthian stance, with which I have great sympathy. One of the most important aspects of the function of poetry in Welsh society as I understand it is that of the poet as celebrator, commemorator, praiser of people and, indeed, also of landscape, also of life itself. My instincts are fundamentally those of somebody who wants to praise and celebrate and commemorate, all my instincts run very strongly in that direction. Because of the nature of my position as an English poet both in England and in Wales, they come up against some very difficult obstacles. And I would tend to see my poetry very much as that of someone who has the strong instincts of a praise poet and who's looking for a form and a way in which these can find expression, and who's therefore struggling with all the considerable obstacles against this happening, obstacles which arise to a large extent from that condition of alienation and estrangement we've already mentioned.

—*So the idea of the poet in the Welsh tradition then is very reinforcing for you personally?*

—Yes, but at the same time I have a lively awareness of the danger of romanticizing the position of the Welsh poet. I mean doubtless if we look at particular modern Welsh poets, we'll find in some of them at least a good deal of torment and a good deal of struggle with difficulties, and I think that's probably in the nature of the art. But certainly it's true to say that the artists I most admire, and I use that word here to encompass the practitioners of other arts as well as poets — those that I most admire are struggling, in different ways, to get out of the clichéd position of alienation so much in our Western culture places them in. Because this notion of the poet as an alienated person is often imposed from the outside, although some write more or less blithely out of this would-be tormenting condition.

—*Basically, this is a matter of relationship, how one relates to one's material, one's world, and the convention of alienation provides one ready-made attitude. But what is sometimes important in a poet's work is the working out of a new relationship, and this can be a major substance of the poetry itself. How do you see your own relation to the landscapes you write about, do you have a position formulated over a period of time from which you write with some security, or is this still a matter of struggle or development?*

—Yes and no. Yes, in the sense that I have strong feelings about the particular landscapes and places I've written about, and insofar as I have strong feelings, then I have a sense of direction, and therefore some sense of security in my subject matter and my attitudes towards it. No, emphatically, in the sense that all my writing, critical writing as well as poetry, is essentially exploratory. If I knew exactly what I wanted to say, if I knew exactly what I felt and thought, indeed if I knew exactly what I had seen or was seeing before writing a poem, I don't think there would be a need to write it. I find out what I want to say, what I think and feel and see in the process of writing and sometimes, rereading poems later on, I see in them what I hadn't seen at the time of composing them.

There is a quotation from David Jones I use when talking about poetry or giving a poetry reading. For me it is the most succinct expression of what I understand the nature of poetry to be. He said in his preface to *The Anathemata*, 'One is trying to make a shape out of the very things of which one is oneself made.' Well, the poet is, of course, trying to make a shape, that's primary; in that respect poetry is craft in which you make a shape out of your words and rhythms, you make something that has an objective existence — what does the poet make a shape out of but the very things of which he is himself made? Now by 'the very things' I understand everything that has shaped him as a human being and, above all, everything that he most feels and most cares for — and they can be things he feels negatively, things that have harmed him as well as things that have had a positive effect. This again immediately places the poet within a particular society and a particular culture, because none of us is made in a vacuum, the things that make us are the things that compose us as social beings in particular places.

But in that poetry is exploratory, is an act of discovery, I find I have come to see more and more of what the things that have made me are in the process of time. One discovers in the process of time, and with me above all in the process of writing, what those things are within one's culture, within one's place, the particular forces, the human forces — or the non-human ones that are present in nature and in landscape. It follows from this, that self-knowledge in relation to the things of which we're composed is something that we gain, if at all, in time. And if some of us gain this through making shapes out of these very things, then our relationship to the things, to the landscape, to the place, is going to be a changing one. Because one's going to see more, or one hopes to, as time passes, and at any given time, one's vision is necessarily partial and includes the possibility of error that is present in all partial seeing. So for that reason I would certainly hope that my relationships with the things I write about are changing, developing ones. This would also be so in that life itself is a continual process of change and that any static attitude in a poet must, I think, lead to rhetoric, and to a stereotyped, and indeed bad, form of writing. I think there is a necessary emotional fluidity, and to some extent a fluidity of thought and attitude in any poet who's going to develop at all. On the one hand it's important to have a sense of direction, but at the same time you don't want the sense of direction to be so comprehensive that you can see the goal before you've arrived at it, because that, too, would negate the necessity for writing poetry, or if it didn't, it would lead to bad poetry.

— *You mentioned the importance of a sense of place earlier, what exactly does the idea of place mean to you?*

—For me, places are not just the buildings or the people who are living there. A place is a totality, a place is all that has created it through the process of time, it is the history, the geology, the circumambient environment, and in addition to that, it is the connection within a single compass of all those living forces. Therfore place, properly understood, is a very complex and living matter.

— *Do you think a preoccupation with place can run the danger of provincialism, which is a criticism often lodged against poetry that looks at the immediate and is concerned with particular places?*

—Yes, it can run that danger, but on the other hand, I'm very suspicious of the word 'provincial' and its normal usage. It's very often used, for example, by the most narrow people, that is to say those who are locked up in the fairly small world of the metropolis, or of the Oxbridge-London triangle, whose sense of the variety of Britain, and the difference of places, the differences of experience within these islands is a very limited one. So I say whenever you hear the word 'provincial', look first of all to see who's using it and try to get some sense of what they mean by it — whether they're using it in a thoughtful way at all, or just as a third-hand perjorative expression. But I would use Patrick Kavanagh's fine definition of the provincial in contrast to the parochial, and to substitute for your word provincial parochial in Kavanagh's sense. Kavanagh described the provincial as that from outside a metropolitan or dominant centre which is aping the fashions of that centre, which is trying to be metropolitan at a distance. The parochial, on the other hand, can be described as that which has such confidence in the place where it is that it assumes, rightly, in my opinion, that the experience of that place is centrally human, is no less centrally human than that of any other place. And Kavanagh described Homer as the most parochial of poets in this sense.

Further, I've come increasingly to see a function of the poet as re-expanding or attempting to contribute to the re-expansion and rediscovery of the world in which we live. I think one of the greatest threats to the twentieth century, which is symbolized as well as represented by the threat of nuclear extinction is that of sameness, of uniformity, of seeing all things and all places as if they were one. But the parochial poet can help make the world larger again, can help us to breathe, can help us to feel the reality of the world in which we live by dwelling upon the particular, by discovering, or rediscovering the particular. I like to quote Roy Fisher, who wrote of Birmingham, 'Most of this has never been seen', which takes us back again to seeing. I think there's a close relationship between seeing, place, and therefore the parochial, and that we can help to return a sense of wonder to the world, a sense of vitality to existence, a sense of reality to place by seeing closely the places that we know and in which we live. It should also be said that a great regard for the parochial, a great regard for the things of which the individual has been made in a particular place contains within it a respect for all places, and in that sense also the world is expanded. Drawing attention to the reality of any one particular place does something rather similar for all other places.

*—Perhaps it's one of the few ways it's possible for some sense of pluralism to survive.*

—That's true, I think a great enemy of the poet — also a great enemy of the human being — which the poet can either help to defeat or cooperate with — is conventional seeing. The images that are imposed upon places from the outside, the images for example, that are placed upon the world by the dominant systems, by nuclear confrontation, to take the largest instance of all, but from that, right down through conventional image-making in the various media, the false image imposed upon the reality of places and people is something all writers should be contending with.

NIGEL JENKINS was born into a farming family on the Gower peninsula in 1949. He worked as a newspaper reporter in the Midlands until 1972, when he travelled in Europe and North Africa. Having studied film and literature at Essex University he travelled in America, but has now settled in Wales again, where he lectures and is involved in the Welsh Union of Writers. He has published a number of pamphlets, and two longer collections of poems, *Song and Dance* (1981) and *Practical Dreams* (1983).

# An Interview with Nigel Jenkins

*—I'd like to ask first how your poems about farm life are related to your development as a poet.*
—They are still the earliest poems I wrote that I regard now as of any use. Derivative in some ways as they might be of one or two influences at the time, they do represent a genuine and fairly simple response to actual lived experience. For the first time in my poetry I dropped my 'poetical' pretences and connected with things that actually happened in childhood. I really enjoyed the process of working very slowly on those poems and discovering quite a lot about that gone world of childhood. I can't imagine having developed without writing them. They were the start of a far more rooted way of going about things.

*—Is the idea of rootedness still important to you?*
—Very much so. I started writing the farm poems when I was at Essex University, totally removed from my former experience. But oddly, that distance from Wales, over there on the east coast of England was a very useful perspective to have on the past. It was then that I started to re-engage with the place, after many years absence, physical and mental, from Wales. And my childhood was very important in my development as a writer because of the connections with the farming community. My father, my brother and I would often go to agricultural shows all over west Wales and meet the farmers. On Tuesdays, every Tuesday with staggering monotony actually, we'd go to Gowerton market where my father worked as an auctioneer, and I got to know the farming community really well.

I came from a very English-speaking area of Gower, but there were a lot of Welsh speakers at the markets. So I had an early awareness of Wales as a bilingual nation, although the tendency of my family was a little bit to despise Welsh language culture, because of their history which was typical of a successful middle-class family coming from Welsh-speaking Wales to Swansea and deciding, very consciously indeed, to chuck the language.

*—What led to your attitudes changing from theirs, for you to affirm a Welsh consciousness and interest in the language?*
—Thinking about Wales. Not taking it for granted. Because I don't think that anybody, whether they speak Welsh or English can any longer take Wales for granted. You have to struggle for Wales all the time, and for your relationship with it. No longer can people be unconsciously Welsh, it's something that has to be maintained as a personal commitment first of all.

*—Was there a definite time when you came to feel this way?*
—I think it came during my time of travelling. I travelled a lot for about ten months after leaving my job on a newspaper, and had some very exciting brushes with other cultures. My experience until then for five or six years had been very English, I had been in the Midlands, only coming back to Wales for holidays. But that's a visitor's relationship with the country, useless really. Travelling around Europe and North Africa, meeting all sorts of people, not only people from the cultures I was visiting, but also fellow-travellers, I found people very interested in the varieties of culture in Europe generally, and some were interested in Wales — also Scotland and Ireland.

That was important, and then at university I started on an unofficial program of studying Welsh literature.

—*Did you have to devise this yourself, or was there already a program?*

—Oh no, there was nothing. I introduced the Literature Department at Essex University to Dafydd ap Gwilym! They were very disturbed: a major medieval poet we've never heard of? I insisted on writing a twenty page essay on Dafydd ap Gwilym, that forced them to actually read him for the first time in their lives. So it was absolutely a self-devised thing. Also, I was reading *Planet*, which I started picking up when I came home on holiday. It was great for me in the seventies. I felt very sympathetic to its determined idea of Wales in the centre of the world, rather than Oxford or Cambridge or London, and to the openness to other parts of the world, and especially minority cultures. I read *Planet* a great deal, and it turned me on to other things.

—*Such as?*

—Gwyn Williams' *Introduction to Welsh Poetry*, and then I started reading his translations. Also Tony Conran's Penguin selection of Welsh poetry, the Introduction of that book was very important to me. And I started reading other poets who had been doing exciting things in the sixties. I was reading some in the sixties, but my passion then was really for rock music, which is a continuing influence for me. But it was in the seventies that the Welsh interest began to surface.

—*To what extent do you consider your own writing to be in a tradition that could be called Anglo-Welsh, especially as you're young enough to have been influenced not only by Welsh poets writing early in this century, but also those who have been writing very recently?*

—I tend to connect with Emyr Humphreys' coolness toward 'Anglo-Welsh' as a tag. As to Welsh poets that were an influence — I liked the poets with a public presence, who could address themselves to a live audience, people like Harri Webb and John Tripp. They were doing readings, they were talking to people, they were going out and saying, well, here's me talking to you. That, I think, is certainly part of the Welsh tradition of social engagement, of the poet among his people — unfortunately you can't quite say 'her' people because women have been squeezed out all down the line until very recently. But this kind of direct contact was important to me because I was, anyway, politically interested and engaged. Other writers I admire include people like Idris Davies and Roland Mathias and of a younger generation, Chris Torrance, Jeremy Hooker, Janet Dubé, Robert Minhinnick. Quite a range of people all doing rather different things, but their influence has been mostly in terms of their outlook on Wales, and their relation to their audience. My interest in terms of technique lay elsewhere. I've enjoyed Tripp for his deep historical interests, but also because he's one of the few people who have connected fairly and squarely with a modern view. His openess to European and American writers and his unaffected way of addressing his audience were attractive to me. David Jones I've been very excited by as well. I read *In Parenthesis* in about 1973. The historical layering of that book was important and exciting to me. Then I read *The Anathemata*, which is a book you can turn to again and again and mine all sorts of wonderful things from it.

—*What are some important non-Welsh interests for you?*

—A wide range of poets, mostly European and American. Neruda, who was perhaps a rather bad influence, since I did go through a spell of being rather sat on by his influence. Vallejo is another Latin American who matters to me and in Spain, Lorca. In Germany, Brecht and Enzensberger. In America, William Carlos Williams, for *Paterson* especially, and Snyder and, just recently, Laurie Anderson. Scotland has produced great stuff this century: MacDiarmid, Sorley Maclean and, giving a very different Glaswegian slant on things, Tom Leonard. In England I go for the 'unofficial' poets — Adrian Mitchell, Lee Harwood, Barry MacSweeney. It's rare to find a poet who really excites me, who becomes my obsession as a reader for long periods, but the Breton poet Guillevic is a happy discovery.

—*What is it about him in particular that attracts you?*

—I like the sense of co-participation as a human being with other entities in the world, maybe animal, maybe mineral. It's akin to some of the writing I've enjoyed from America which has been influenced by Japanese and Oriental styles. Snyder, for example, has the same attitude as Guillevic in not putting the human interest in a superior relation to the interest of other beings and things. The thingness of Guillevic I find very interesting, the way in which an ordinary artefact like a hammer or a nail can be writen about in a few simple words and you'll never think the same about a hammer or a nail after reading those few lines. In other words, he is a changer. And I do believe art changes you as a reader or a listener and therefore that it changes the world, because you are a changed component in the world after you have been changed by reading such and such a poem.

—*So do you see a direct — or indirect — relation between art and politics?*

—I think there have been effective political poems, Wales is full of political poems, and it's possible for people to have too high an expectation of what they can do. Now, after the failure of devolution in Wales the overtly political poetry leading up to the vote seems sometimes rather complacent.

—*And perhaps dated as well?*

—Yes, but I think there is a space for a poetry whose life is short and which attempts to make an intervention — not, often, on a specifically political plane by actually changing people's voting habits, but it can contribute to a political climate. In any case, even non-political poetry, by adopting a 'non-political' stance adopts a political attitude. You can't get away from it. It's nonsense to talk of anything that's non-political. Politics is to do with how we organise our lives together and writing has to do with saying, and as soon as we open our mouths the saying is communicating, is involving itself with the political.

—*Are there connections for you between the issue of the survival of Welsh and Anglo-Welsh culture and the larger question of survival on the planet?*

—Yes, because to me the existence of these wholly obscene weapons, weapon systems — ways of thinking, that's the important thing — does represent a direct threat to all that is gentle, tender, complex with us as human beings. A lot of that gentleness is bound up with how we've developed our ways of living through various societies, languages, cultural habits. And the more we lose our grip on these necessary cultural differences and separatenesses, the more we slip towards a way of thinking, an attitude to life that is prepared in fact finally to junk them with a big bang.

I think it's not totally coincidental that the Greenham Common action started in Wales and that Wales is the first country in the world to go nuclear-free. Now that's been described by some as yet another flatulent Welsh gesture, that is, unless it's actually backed up with continuing action, continuing commitment to what that title, 'nuclear-free zone' means. But even as a title, a designation, it matters and it was an important component in the refusal to take part in Operation Hard Rock, the civil defence operation whereby the Government expected all local councils to participate in preparing for nuclear war on a local level. But so many councils refused that they had to abandon it. This was a tremendous victory for the anti-nuclear movement, and Wales was very strongly behind that.

—*In a poem like 'Snowdrops', your political concerns seem quite connected, or interwoven, with aspects of your immediate experience and environment.*

—First, I should really say that I didn't set out to write a 'political' poem, this poem really came about as the result of an insistent need to understand why it was important to me to go out and pick snowdrops every year.

—*Is this something you did as a child?*

—Yes, I suppose we had always picked snowdrops. Year after year, I was finding myself going back to the little wood on my family's farm. If I didn't find any snowdrops, I would return home disappointed, and if I did find them, conversely, it was an occasion for delight.

One year I picked a beautiful handful and decided to try and write something about them and failed. So I put the poem away for a year and maybe the next year, too, didn't manage much. It was a two or three year spell with a couple of false starts; one or two sections of the poem partly existed. My first thought, in the first part of the poem, was that in picking the snowdrops I was involved in some kind of magic activity, advancing the spring if you like, but in a deeper way than just to do with the weather, because most people are pretty low in the extremely cold weather of January. So actually possessing the snowdrops seemed to me to be like having a hold on spring, on the prospect of changing the depressing conditions of that time of year. There was a connection in my mind with the old Lascaux and Font de Gaume cave paintings, and the mostly guessed at rituals of those early cave painters. We understand, as far as we can, that they were involved in a form of imitative magic by drawing these animals, putting them in some way within their orbit of influence. I felt my drive to pick snowdrops was somehow related to that. The idea of this tentative kinship between myself and those early cavers raised the whole question of the year itself, from thinking about how human beings had survived in that particular place in France over the centuries, the millennia, and naturally Paviland Man came to mind.

I was living at the time half way between Paviland and Port Talbot, two very representative poles. I thought of Paviland as a place of great darkness, because we know so little about Paviland Man, his society, the men and women of early caving days, at least eighteen thousand years ago. So there was all this uncertainty, but also a tremendous strength that I located there, strength in terms of the determination to survive, because those people were the first who developed the technology to live in those horrifyingly cold conditions, on the edge of the great ice field. When all the other animals had left for other climates, they had developed enough to sustain themselves there. Then, looking east, there was the ambiguous light of Port Talbot, which doesn't come into the poem, with that orange sky flaring, often, at night as they release the gases and open the furnaces. And I felt an uncertainty or conflict as to what that represents, in terms of the south Wales communities who need it economically to survive, and also in terms of how it suggest what technology offers us now — total obliteration if we blow it, which I fear we might well do. So the double edged nature of technology enters in, the tiny technology those people at Paviland were developing, and the modern ones which seem so necessary and hugely threatening. As for the poem's other concerns there is a question of actually writing or saying, the uncertainty, always, of being able to continue to speak to any effect. Then poverty also concerns me, because I've always felt, as many other people do, that the nuclear issue is tied up so totally with the fact that staggering numbers of children — several millions — die of starvation every year. Thinking about this question of world starvation is equally as dizzying as thinking about the nuclear threat, the scale of it is so massive, and we in the wealthy nations are so thoroughly implicated. One other thing is the problem of how we, as human beings, treat each other. On the whole I'm a fairly optimistic person. I believe in good and see it around me all the time, but I'm also aware every day just in reading the newspaper the kind of atrocity mentioned in the poem. So in the poem I was aware of that immediate destructive potential in us as a real threat, alongside the nuclear threat. But the poem does eventually end on an optimistic note. I originally wrote 'the year will survive', but a little pessimism entered in, and I wrote 'may' instead.

ANNE STEVENSON was born in England in 1933, but grew up and was educated in America. Her volumes of poetry include *Reversals* (1969), *Travelling Behind Glass* (1974), *Enough of Green* (1977) and most recently *Minute by Glass Minute* (1982). The poems in this last book were mostly written while she was living in Hay-on-Wye, where she ran a poetry bookshop with Michael Farley. She went on to become Literary Fellow at Durham and Newcastle Universities (1981-82), and she still lives near Durham.

# An Interview with Anne Stevenson

—*First of all, how did your experience of Wales affect your poetry?*

—I would say it affected it profoundly. We came to Wales from Oxford, leaving academia behind. I've always felt ambiguous about academia because I was brought up in an academic household in America. I've tried successively in my life and work to get away from too much dependence on the cerebral. So leaving Oxford for Wales was, in a sense, an act of faith. But I was unprepared for the shock, the visionary shock of the Wye valley. The poems I wrote in Hay didn't happen until the second or third year of being there. At first I wrote nothing. Hay, of course, is a border community between Hereford and Wales, and I knew very little about Wales when we went to live there. But my antennae quickly picked up a sense of the Welshness of Wales — the Welsh landscape, the Welsh character, even the Welsh language, though I never learned it. All this was something entirely unEnglish. Celtic. A Celticness, related to what I felt living in Scotland some years before. Possibly I was particularly open to Wales because I was happy in Hay. When you cease to be ravenous for notice or money, and when you've found the right person to live with, then you're open to the outside. I was wide open in Hay, so Welshness and Wales poured in on me.

Of course, I'm aware that there's a petty-minded side to the Welsh, a chapelish narrowness, sometimes, a blackness which can be oppressive. The Welsh know this themselves. But in Hay I read the *Mabinogion* and as much else as I could find in translation of Welsh literature, and I was excited, feeling that this was a new country, part of Britain and yet totally unknown to me. There is that in the Welsh which is suspicious of outsiders. The Welsh are embattled in their language and customs, and they are right to feel embattled. But they are of a nation that cares enormously for poetry and music, and in this way they seem to run counter to the tide of contemporary civilization which is sinking under the mire of commercialism and cheapness and vulgarity. So I found the Welsh emphasis on learning, poetry and music to be nourishing, like bread to the starving.

—*Landscape has been an important element in your poetry, though obviously you don't write from the perspective of having been settled in one place all your life, since you're American. Nevertheless, you seem to have a very intimate connection with landscape. How would you describe this relationship to landscape and its role in your work?*

—Ever since I can remember, where I am has been important to me. I've always liked the sea and the deepest kind of countryside, although I do find that the city provides energies, too — city landscapes, docks, railways, any kind of working landscape, even the collieries of the North-East. Their ugliness is what is interesting. But I'm drawn to natural landscapes as a moth is drawn to the candle. I like light; I don't like dark places. Light, reflections, water, glass get into my poems without my knowing how. I don't think my poems are *paysages moralisés* — I don't try to draw sermons from stones — but I do depend on the spirit of place a lot. I have to feel in tune with places before I can write in them. I think places have as much personality as people; I feel about places as I feel about people, the same kind of love, awe, or repulsion.

*—So is it more difficult for you to write in places that are not welcoming, that are hostile to your particular needs?*

—It depends on what I'm writing. I find it difficult to write poems in places that have no personality: middle-class well-heeled suburbs, for instance, or in contemporary institutional architecture — tiny office-boxes. An old tenement or a falling-down barn is preferable. When people impose upon landscape a characterless kind of conformity, when landscape is deprived of its humanity and the feeling of people having lived there — made history there — then they deprive it of spirit — and of the possibility of language.

*—As a British-American, did 'Green Mountain, Black Mountain', represent some kind of attempt to unify your own experience?*

—Naturally, although I didn't set out consciously to do that. In the spring of 1980 I went to America to do some readings. I wrote the first section in New England and then wondered where it was going to lead me; but it was spring 1981 before I knew how to continue. I was walking in Wales when the lines 'Rain in the wind/ and the green need of again/ opening in this Welsh wood' just appeared, you know, the way lines are given to you. And I thought, maybe what I can do with those strange American lines is to contrast them with these new Welsh lines. The poem came together in a week after that. It's interesting that in England I've had a very bad press on 'Green Mountain, Black Mountain'. Most English critics don't read by ear — don't care, apparently, about how a poem sounds. The Welsh and the Americans, on the other hand, seem to like the poem. Writing it convinced me that I am not, after all, an English poet. My affinity with Wales is American. Then, of course, the poem is about resurrection, a subject which embarrasses the intellectual English — about the kind of resurrection that happens in life, again and again. A part of your past seems to go out of existence, to die. And then it returns and you see the present in a new perspective. This is what I mean by resurrection in life, life itself as a resurrecting phenomenon.

The two poets I most admire in England are Peter Redgrove and Geoffrey Hill; neither is afraid of 'ambition' and they write about things that matter. Otherwise I am more drawn to the Celtic, — the Irish, Scottish and Welsh view of things. But the American war of independence still goes on in me, except that sometimes it's a civil war between my two halves. You said it yourself; being an American in Britain is like being a schizophrenic with an entire ocean between the hemispheres of the brain. But the tension, although exhausting, has at least helped me not to repeat myself. Poetry is, for me at least, an investigative art, a pilgrimage. In exploring one's life — not private life, but experience *of* life — a pattern of discovery, of reconciliation, of meaning does emerge *as* language. The language of poetry doesn't *express* meaning, it *is* the meaning. It would have been easy to have written 'Green Mountain, Black Mountain' as a reminiscence, autobiography, confession. But to find my own feeling about my parents (the poem is an elegy to their memory) the language had to be as complex as that feeling. Their personalities had to be suggested by sound and topography and history, not by recollected incidents.

*—Do you think history and myth have a particular attraction for you because of your own history of pilgrimage and mobility?*

—What is myth if it doesn't define experience? Myth is what we all share, myth has to be a living part of language, otherwise we have nothing in common to refer to. Despite the awfulness of superficial civilization, myths don't pass. They go underground and resurrect as our lives re-enact them. All the great stories — love stories, stories of revenge, ambition, the rise and fall of the great, the helplessness of man in time — all the Greek stories, the Biblical stories, Shakespeare's plots — they are archetypal. There are not many ways in which to deviate from them. I believe you can find substantiation for the archetypal theory in the works of Carl Jung, though I hadn't read Jung when I first began to suspect there were only three or four stories behind everything we do. But of course Jung makes sense. You don't have to go in for woolly metaphysics to see that a poet's job (not the philosopher's) is to unearth and reveal the myths we live... the *symbols*, if you like. I don't see that it's pretentious for a poet to speak of or through symbols. Yeats did, Eliot did, Auden did, though he often pretended not to.

*—I wonder if your sense of myth is at all related to the way you see the physical world. For instance, the flowers of 'Himalayan Balsam' are very immediate and sensuous in their presence — they seem to function as a kind of transparency; and the meditation they provoke is not separate from their physicality.*

—True. I don't see nature as metaphorical, if you want to put it that way. Your word 'transparent' is better. The last poem in *Minute by Glass Minute* is called 'Transparencies', and although that is a more complex poem than I can explain here, my hope was that the glass image in 'Buzzard and Alder' and that in 'Transparencies' would begin and end the book, suggesting that experience is at once transparent, like glass, and reflective, like glass. I think human experience is like this. Take the surrealistic effect you get when looking through a window at night. You can see through the glass to the trees or buildings outside; at the same time you also see your face, or really, through your face. This 'surrealism of everyday life' as Elizabeth Bishop called it, is obsessive with me. I can't escape the fact that my first English collection was called *Travelling Behind Glass*, and this one, *Minute by Glass Minute*. It's hard to discuss these things, but I do believe that this transparency of nature is what mystics of all religions have meant when they spoke of the radiance of God. People will and do deny that such transparency, such radiance exists, but I can't deny it because I've experienced it.

*—As a poet writing in the 'eighties', what uses do you see for poetry today, in the kind of world we live in?*

—Of course, poetry has lots of uses. I would never say that poetry should not be entertainment — even in the 'kind of world we live in'. Heaven knows we need to laugh. But I feel *some* poetry, at least, must find its way to people's hearts — their individual hearts. Poets must try to speak of the spirit to the spirit, to the desolate, the lost, to those bogged down in consumer materialism and to those who are allowed to have no part in consumer well-being. All that people really want has, perhaps, to be unobtainable. And poetry happens rarely. I mean, the words on the page aren't the poem. The poem is the moment of interchange between words and mind, or lines and reader. The reader re-creates what is written, and only then is it a poem to him.

So poetry makes things happen, but inwardly — it never changes the outward world. When it attempts to, it becomes rhetoric, propaganda. It's for this reason that I oppose much of the poetry of the women's movement, although I am sympathetic with its aims. Ban-the-bomb poetry, too, assumes too much 'attitude'; it can't afford the luxury of a double focus, of seeing more than one side. Yet I think poetry can wake people up and show them what matters is making and thinking. People are not happy simply as observers and seizers, taking from life; people need to contribute, and they do that when they read poetry fairly, openly. I wish more people would read poems as poems, not as exercises or fearful duties.

— *You've already mentioned Peter Redgrove and Geoffrey Hill as English poets you admire. Who else do you admire? Which poets have you learned from?*

—Well, I admire Seamus Heaney and Ted Hughes, but they're not poets I learn from or instinctively turn to, as I turn to Yeats, constantly back to Yeats, and recently to Villon, recently to Marvell, to Herbert, to Emily Dickinson. I don't feel one should stick oneself in one's own time. I read poetry all the time, but change poets frequently. Elizabeth Bishop was an 'influence' for a long time in the 60's, as was Marianne Moore. I might say that Sylvia Plath who'd died by the time I'd begun writing, was little more than a heavy cloud on the horizon until I re-read her poems recently and realized what a marvellous technician she was. Like Gillian Clarke, she was what I call a 'projective sensibility'; that is, her psychological power was so strong and her execution in poetry was so persuasive that it is hard to read her poems without being bowled over. Yet one doesn't feel that objects in themselves had any great significance to her. *She* gave things significance. I'm not saying that's a bad thing. But it's the opposite of Keats' Negative Capability — it's projecting egotistical capability on the neutral things of this world, magnifying, glorifying — as Dylan Thomas did, and Wallace Stevens. Perhaps I am making too much of this, but it seems to me that a poet like Gillian Clarke differs from poets like Roland Mathias and Jeremy Hooker in something of the same way. In Gillian's poems you are always aware of Gillian writing; she sucks up her impressions and gives them back stamped with her voice. In Roland you hear or overhear many voices — historical, geographical, so there is often a question as to where Roland is. Jeremy has written himself on the importance of 'place' to him. His impersonality is his strength. Which is not to say either Roland or Jeremy lack voices; it's that they do their best to convert their mirrors into windows. Their poems have a terrifying integrity, much harder for a reader to come to terms with than more personally immediate poems.

— *What direction do you want your poetry to go in now?*

—The way I *want* it to go and the way it *does* go may be different things. I should like to return to the narrative method of *Correspondences* again; I've had rather too much of myself recently and am thinking of a play. To me poetry and religion have a common root — 'In the Beginning was the Word'; to contemplate a body of poetry without a religious core seems to me impossible. The concepts of imagination and faith have to be re-examined — not pedantically but morally. I expect I'm a true puritan at heart. I can't live in a meaningless world; I can't accept that everything's as absurd as it seems on the surface — or rather, it seems to me that the poet and the priest are alike in that they are committed to refuting any overall theory of the absurd. In the finding or making of patterns of language a poet finds his or her purpose; that's the fun of it all, and the torment, too.

# Notes

## ROLAND MATHIAS

19. ROLAND MATHIAS in his garden at Brecon (IW/RW).
20. BARAFUNDLE BAY, South of Pembroke (SB).
21. Gwyther Street and Llanion are in Pembroke Dock, where Roland Mathias used to live.
22. DUNES AT FRESHWATER WEST, near Pembroke (IW).
23. socius: ally.
25. BRAMBLES (SB).
26. ICICLES (RW).
27. Soar: a hamlet north of Brecon.
    Struwwelpeter: a naughty boy in a German fairy tale who let his fingernails grow too long, thereby incurring dire punishment.
28. NEAR THE SOURCE OF THE USK, MYNYDD DU (RW).
30. BRECHFA CHAPEL, above Llyswen, between Brecon and Hay (IW).
33. IN THE GRAVEYARD OF BRECHFA CHAPEL (SB/IW).
34. TALYBONT RESERVOIR, Brecon Beacons (RW).
35. Caerfanell, Grwyney and Senni are all tributaries of the River Usk. The church of Partrishow (Patricio) is to the east of Crickhowell.
36. cenedl: tribe.
    tallut: Gower version of the Welsh taflawd – hayloft.
    rhos: moor.
    milgis: greyhounds.
37. ABOVE TYLORSTOWN, RHONDDA FACH (IW).
38. PORTH CWYFAN, Anglesey (RW).
39. St. Beuno miraculously replaced the head of St. Winifred after she had been decapitated by Caradoc, Prince of Wales. The event is supposed to have happened at Holywell, Clwyd.
40. TOMBSTONE, PORTH CWYFAN (RW).

## ROBERT MINHINNICK

42. ROBERT MINHINNICK in the graveyard of Smyrna Baptist Chapel, Pen-y-Fai (RW).
45. THE POET'S GRANDFATHER, IVOR THOMAS, in his garden (RW).
48. SMITH'S GARAGE, NOW DERELICT, HEOL EGLWYS, PEN-Y-FAI (IW).
49. THE WORKBENCH INSIDE THE GARAGE (RW).
50. ORCHARD AT PEN-Y-FAI, close by the one referred to in the poem, which has been replaced by a car park (SB).
53. NANT FFORNWG, near Pen-y-Fai (IW).

55. THE DISUSED BOATHOUSE AT COURT COLMAN, near Pen-y-Fai (IW).
56. MARGAM ABBEY (SB/IW).
57. Llywelyn Siôn was a sixteenth-century scribe associated with Margam Abbey.
    Llangewydd is near Pen-y-fai.
59. SKER POINT, near Porthcawl (RW).
60. BLOCK OF FLATS AT HIRWAUN (SB/IW).
61. Rhigos is a village and mountain near Hirwaun.


## JOHN TRIPP

64. JOHN TRIPP with Rodin's 'Lovers' in the National Museum of Wales, Cardiff (IW).
66. Eglwys Newydd is the Welsh name for Whitchurch, the Cardiff suburb where John Tripp lives. The village of Tongwynlais is to the north.
    D.P.s: Displaced Persons.
    Rowland Lee: an English bishop appointed by Henry VIII as Lord President of the Marches in 1534 and known for his virulently anti-Welsh views.
    Dic Penderyn: a Welsh worker hung in Cardiff goal in 1831, in the aftermath of the Merthyr Rising.
67. THE A470 THROUGH WHITCHURCH. At the top of the picture is Castell Coch, on the hillside above Tongwynlais (IW).
69. THE WELSH OFFICE, CARDIFF (IW).
70. PENARTH. The burnt-out shell of the Esplanade Hotel is on the right (IW).
71. Bargoed, where John Tripp was born, is a mining town in the Rhymney Valley.
73. BARRY ISLAND (IW).
74. THE FORMER MINING VILLAGE OF GILFACH GOCH (IW).
75. The Six Bells is a now ruined inn in the valley, and the Britannic was one of the main mines.
76. Senghenydd: another mining village, site of a notorious disaster.
77. GILFACH GOCH (IW).
78. CONTI'S CAFE, BUILTH WELLS (IW).
79. Cwmowen is a small settlement on the Mynydd Epynt, a bleak upland to the west of Builth Wells.
80. Aber: Aberystwyth.
81. PLWMP, on the road between Cardigan and Aberystwyth (IW).
82. BOSHERSTON CHURCH (IW).
83. Author's note: Near the ancient village of Bosherston on the South Pembroke coast, the lily ponds are so old that no-one has been able to fix the date of their forming.
84. BOSHERSTON PONDS (SB/IW).

## GILLIAN CLARKE

86. GILLIAN CLARKE (IW).
88. CALFARIA CHAPEL, LOGIN (SB/IW).
90. Taid: North Walian for grandfather.
91. THE RIVER MELLTE, near Ystradfellte (RW).
92. Mamgu: grandmother.
    pais: petticoat.
93. 19TH CENTURY THREADWORK TABLECLOTH belonging to the poet (SB/RW).
95. WELSH DRESSER in the poet's house in Cardiff (RW).
97. BARLEY FIELD, CARDIGANSHIRE (RW).
100. COTTAGES, BETTWS-Y-COED (RW).
101. Nain: North Walian for grandmother.
     Ceredigion: Cardigan.
103. Diaconydd: deacon.
     Trysorydd: treasurer.
104. Dŵr: water.
105. WATER (RW).
107. BUZZARD SKULL belonging to the poet (SB/RW).
108. THE SITE OF THE DEMOLISHED EAST MOORS STEELWORKS, CARDIFF (IW).
109. Penylan, Roath and Rumney are suburbs of Cardiff.

## JEREMY HOOKER

General note: Jeremy Hooker's poems are set in the area of the hill-range Mynydd Bach, south of Aberystwyth. The Beidog is a small river flowing down off the hill and Trefenter is a settlement on the hillside.

111. JEREMY HOOKER on Mynydd Bach (SB/IW).
112. THE RIDGE OF MYNYDD BACH (SB).
114. Taliesen: an early, semi-legendary Welsh poet.
115. AFON BEIDOG (RW).
116. BRYNBEIDOG, the poet's former home (SB).
117. Er Cof: in memory.
119. A STONE, ORIGINALLY INTENDED AS A GRAVESTONE, WHICH IS IN THE FLOOR OF BRYNBEIDOG (SB/IW).
120. LLYN EIDDWEN, ON MYNYDD BACH (RW).
123. RUINS BY LLYN EIDDWEN (RW).
125. SHEEP'S WOOL (RW).
127. HAYFIELD BELOW MYNYDD BACH (SB).
128. BESIDE THE BEIDOG in the fields below Mynydd Bach (SB).
130. FOXGLOVE, MYNYDD BACH (SB).

## NIGEL JENKINS

133. NIGEL JENKINS at Horton, Gower (RW).
135. MAIDENHAIR FERN belonging to the poet (RW).
136. ABOVE THREE CLIFFS BAY, GOWER (SB/IW).
138. FIELD AND COPSE ON THE FARM WHERE NIGEL JENKINS GREW UP, Pennard, Gower (SB).
140. INSIDE THE COPSE (SB).
143. SNOWDROPS (RW).
144. Author's note: tlws yr eira etc. are five Welsh expressions signifying snowdrops.
146. THE COAST AT PAVILAND, GOWER. Goat's Hole Cave is the indentation, top right (SB).
147. GOAT'S HOLE CAVE, PAVILAND, viewed from the edge of the sea (IW).
148. Author's note: A cave in Gower in which in 1823, Dr. William Buckland found the skeleton of what he mistakenly took to be a woman. The remains which were stained with red ochre and which had evidently been ritually buried, were discovered in 1922 to be about 18,000 years old. They were, until recently, the oldest human bone find in these islands.
149. THE BONES OF THE 'RED LADY OF PAVILAND', now stored in a drawer in the University Museum, Oxford (SB/IW).
150. Deheubarth: the old word for South West Wales.
    Brawdy: R.A.F. base and American submarine tracking station in western Dyfed.
151. CASTELL CARREG CENNEN (IW).
152. i.m. 1.3.79 : on March 1st, 1979, the people of Wales voted in a referendum four to one against a measure of increased autonomy through the establishment of a Welsh Assembly.
    hwyl: untranslatable, but suggesting gusto.
    Ar hyd y nos, ar hyd y dydd: all through the night, all through the day.
    S.A.: Special Ale produced by the Cardiff brewery Brains, familiarly known as 'skull attack'.
153. POSTERS IN PEMBROKE (IW).


## ANNE STEVENSON

155. ANNE STEVENSON and Guinesss on the banks of the Wye (SB).
156. HIMALAYAN BALSAM (SB).
160. THE WYE AT HAY (RW).
161. DETAIL, THE WYE (RW).
162. THE BLACK MOUNTAINS (RW).
163. mowin: Vermonters term for hayfield.

164. King Arthur and his warriors are, in Welsh legend, said not to be dead but asleep in a cave. At a peal of a bell, they will arise to rescue Wales from her oppressors when her need is greatest.

165. CRAIG-Y-DDINAS, in the Vale of Neath. Within this rock is one of the supposed sites of Arthur's Cave (IW).

166. WOOD AT CWM-CLŶD, below the Black Mountains (SB).

167. Teirnon and Pryderi are characters associated with horses in the First Branch of the Mabinogion.
    Annwfn or Annwn is the Welsh otherworld. The colours of things and creatures belonging to Annwfn are red and white.

168. The quotations are from William Bradford's History of Plymouth Plantation as quoted by Perry Miller in *The American Puritans* (New York, 1956).

171. THE WYE FROM HAY BRIDGE (SB).

174. RUINED COTTAGE IN CWM-CLŶD WOODS (SB).

177. THE BLACK MOUNTAINS (IW).

Author's general note on 'Green Mountain, Black Mountain':
This poem is dedicated to my parents, both of whom died before the 1980's arrived. My mother was a writer and my father an amateur pianist and cellist.

The portraits accompanying the interviews are all by Susan Butler, except for John Tripp's, which is by Ian Walker.

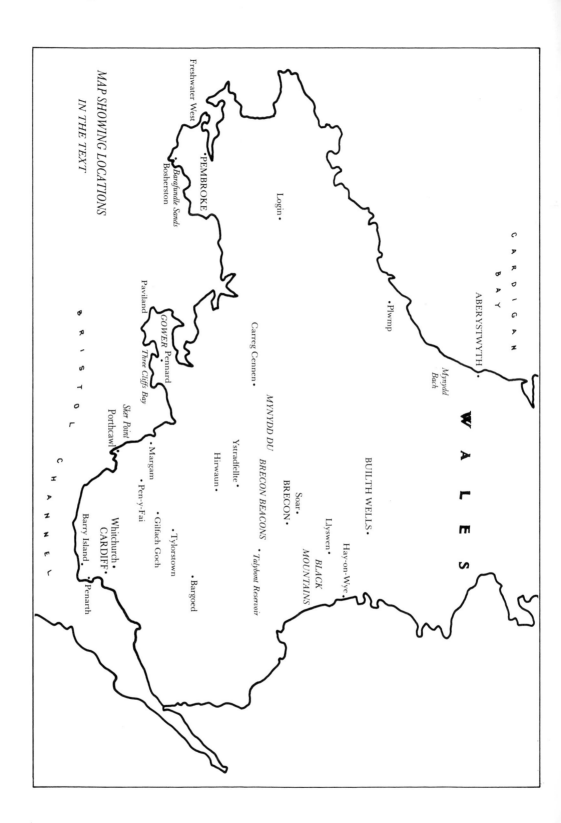

MAP SHOWING LOCATIONS
IN THE TEXT

CARDIGAN BAY

BRISTOL CHANNEL

W A L E S

Freshwater West
•PEMBROKE
Barafundle Sands
Bosherston
Login•
•Plwmp
ABERYSTWYTH •
Mynydd Bach
Paviland
GOWER Pennard
Three Cliffs Bay
Carreg Cennen •
MYNYDD DU
BRECON BEACONS
Ysiradfellte •
Hirwaun •
Sker Point
Porthcawl
• Margam
• Pen-y-Fai
• Gilfach Goch
• Tylorstown
• Bargoed
Whitchurch •
CARDIFF •
Barry Island •
• Penarth
Soar•
BRECON •
• Talybont Reservoir
BUILTH WELLS •
Hay-on-Wye •
Llyswen •
BLACK MOUNTAINS

222

# Biographies

SUSAN BUTLER came to Britain from the U.S.A. in 1980, after completing a Doctorate in Comparative Literature at the University of Massachusetts. She then studied on the Documentary Photography course at Newport, Gwent. She has since exhibited in group shows in Wales, written articles about photography and, in 1983, organised the exhibition, *New Perspectives on the Nude* for the Ffotogallery, Cardiff. She is now co-editor of the magazine *Creative Camera*.

ROSIE WAITE lives in Bethesda, North Wales. Her involvement with photography began while working on an exhibition for environmental groups in Wales. She later studied photography at Newport. Since graduating in 1981, she has exhibited in several shows in Wales and was commissioned by Wildwood House to illustrate a book on the Wye Valley which was published in 1984.

IAN WALKER was born in Birmingham but now teaches at Gwent College, Newport. He has written about art and photography for publications including *The Guardian*, *Art Monthly* and *Creative Camera*, and his photographs have been seen in several one person and group shows. His most recent exhibition *The Other Side of the Castle* toured Wales in 1983-84.

ANTHONY CONRAN was born in India in 1931, but came to North Wales in 1939. He is a Tutor in English at the University College of North Wales, Bangor. His collected translations in *The Penguin Book of Welsh Verse* (1967) established his reputation; several volumes of his own poems have also been published, and his most recent critical work is *The Cost of Strangeness* (1982).

# Acknowledgements

All poems by Roland Mathias are published in *Burning Brambles* (1983, Gwasg Gomer).

Robert Minhinnick: 'Smith's Garage', 'The Orchard', 'The Brook' and 'The Boathouse' are from *Life Sentences* (1983, Poetry Wales Press), the remainder are from *Native Ground* (1979, Christopher Davies Ltd.).

All poems by John Tripp are published in *Collected Poems 1958-1978* (1978, Christopher Davies Ltd.), except 'Scratch Farmer', from *Passing Through* (1984, Poetry Wales Press).

All poems by Gillian Clarke are published in *Letter from a far country* (1982, Carcanet New Press).

All poems by Jeremy Hooker are published in *Englishman's Road* (1980, Carcanet New Press), except 'Leaving' which is uncollected.

All poems by Nigel Jenkins are published in *Song & Dance* (1982, Poetry Wales Press), except 'Snowdrops' and 'Castell Carreg Cennen', published in *Practical Dreams* (1983, Galloping Dog Press).

All poems by Anne Stevenson are published in *Minute by Glass Minute* (1982, Oxford University Press).